Daddy On Board

Tales from the Front Seat, Volume 1

BY CHRISTOPHER SMITH

From columns published in The Leaf-Chronicle newspaper, Clarksville, Tenn.

www.daddyonboard.com

Daddy on Board
Tales from the Front Seat, Volume 1
By Christopher Smith
Illustrations by Timothy Smith

Copyright © 2004 Christopher Smith. All rights reserved.
Printed in the United States of America.

The stories in this book are reprinted herein with the permission of *The Leaf-Chronicle*, for whom they were originally written in 2001, 2002 and 2003.

Additional copies may be ordered at:
www.daddyonboard.com

For reprint or excerpt solicitation, contact:
Christopher Smith by email: smittyco@aol.com

ISBN: 1-4116-1828-9

To Bert Hitchcock,
who told me I could write.

Contents

Foreward: The Daddyhood Movement — ix

Dragons, Dinosaurs and Yaks, Oh My!	1
For Richer, for Poorer, for Pudding	3
End in Sight for Daddy's Trash Burden	5
Baseball Parenting Has Dads in Pickle	7
Six Rules of Life from a 3-Year-Old	9
Demon Child Comes Out in Long Drive	11
Popsicle Sticks and 'Kumbaya'	14
Kid Motto: 'Born to Be Rude'	16
'Gerjus Kur' Takes Detour in Learning	18
Good Dads Chase Rabbits in Pajamas	21
Tough Editor in a Small Package	23
Costumed Daddy a Treat for Young Ghouls	26
Smart Dads Keep Quiet About Treats	28
Why You Should 'Go' Before You Leave	31
Family Tradition Has Way of Making Itself	34
New Year's Resolutions for Dads	36
Lousy Name Part of Job for Top Toys	38
Lingerie Mag a Major Find for a Little Boy	41
Life of Blues Starts with First 'Harlomica'	43
Birth Coach Feels Rusty but Ready	46
Four-Year-Old Checks the Game of Kings	49
Little Mr. Fixit Needs to Work on His Solutions	52
Second Baby Sends Daddy into the Deep End	55
Being a Dad is Snot What You'd Expect	57
Attack of the Sugar Frosted Syrup Smacks	59
World Began Not with Bang, but with Bear	62
Dad's No Good with a Bad Back	65
Cherry Tree Lesson Isn't Working Out	68
There's More to Baby than a 'Goodgie' Face	71
Bad News: Boy's Electric to Blueberries	73

Daddy on Board

Daddy Takes Leap Into Dark Socks	75
Spontaneous Romance? Ha Ha Ha!	77
Conch Tossing a Total Blast for the Boy	79
The Quiet Life Isn't Always by Choice	81
Monsters No Match for Lambie-Pie	84
Rub a Dub-Dub Don't Let Dad Near the Tub	87
Half the Trip Is Getting Out the Front Door	90
Storm Calmed By Questions, Oreos	93
Fox Family Has Exciting Thanksgiving	95
Pay Attention to That Cricket, Boy	98
Real Men Proven on Sledding Hill	101
Devil Chases After Daddy's Perfect Day	103
The Daht Bounces for Pthbbt 'Nah'	105
Melodrama Not Enough to Win Parole	107
Flying Kissinger Foiled Again	110
Family Planning Requires a Plan	112
Danger Girl Puts Parents to Shame	115
Snips, Snails, Plus a Pinch of Jedi Knight	117
Disney Fun in the Ears of Beholder	120
About the Author	125
Acknowledgments	125

Daddy on Board

FOREWARD

The Daddyhood Movement

Confession: I'm a lousy dad. No, really – I'm not just saying that. When I leave my life on cruise control, I spend too much time at work, and when I'm home I spend too little with my kids.

I'm often irritable, and I sometimes scold my children more than I play with them.

But the fact is, if I were the perfect dad, or even a great dad, I could never write a weekly column about fatherhood.

Most of these columns were born out of trial and error, the research and flubbing that amounts to parenting in the millennium: We think we know what's best for our kids, if for no other reason than it's different from what our parents did. But half the time we give our new tricks a shot, they don't work, and we find ourselves calling the grandparents for advice. Half the time, that is.

One thing that's starkly different from the way things were when I was a kid is that what once passed for fatherhood is as long-gone as the rotary phone and smoking in the house. Fathers these days, when they're present, have to be omnipresent. We don't just bring home the bacon, we're expected to cook it, serve it, do the dishes and change the diaper – or at least come close to an equal share of the bacon-frying our wives have been doing for the last couple of centuries.

The flip side of putting behind the era of "Father Knows Best" is the gradual discovery that fathers are best. Despite society's ongoing attempts to make itself feel better about single motherhood, studies keep smacking us in the face with the obvious: Kids need moms and dads. Kids raised without fathers are more likely to flunk a grade in school, to become a criminal, abuse drugs and alcohol, and on, and on, and on.[1]

Us men, who tend to be pretty stupid when faced with the obvious, are beginning to realize we matter to our kids. These days you hear more about stay-at-home dads as a real option and not some sort of "Mr. Mom" joke. When I go to the hardware store with my toddler daughter, I find myself among about a half-dozen dads shopping on their own with kids in the basket, on the shoulders or running down the aisle.

Last year I interviewed a guy for an article who quit his high-intensity management job (and sold his souped-up Camaro dream car) so he could spend more time with his children.

Even my father, who was your typical 1970s dad – working long hours to support his family and taking lots of business trips – has discovered in his late 50s, with the children from his second marriage, that it's more important to play baseball with his sons than it is to mow the grass or bring home work from the office. He, too, has joined what I call the Daddyhood Movement.

Since I started writing this column, I've heard from several men who've joined this informal club. Like the Air Force colonel who told me about having his uniform soiled by a last-minute diaper change before he left for an official function. Or the corporate executive who admitted he gets all teared up reading to his toddler the closing lines of "Guess How Much I Love You."

These aren't superdads. None of us are – but the thing is, we're trying.

And that's basically what *Daddy on Board* is about: My struggle with becoming and being a good dad. It isn't always pretty, and it isn't always pleasant. But more often than not, there's something in it that I can laugh about, even if that something is myself.

---

1. See U.S. Department of Health and Human Services Fatherhood Initiative at http://fatherhood.hhs.gov; or "America's Children in Brief: Key National Indicators of Well-Being 2004" at http://www.childstats.gov

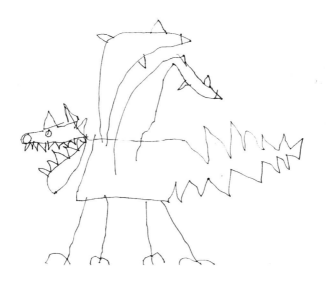

Dragons, Dinosaurs and Yaks, Oh My!

Often when I sit down to write, my 3-year-old takes the silence as an invitation to come tell a story.

"Lasternight, when I was asleep, I heard a dangerous roar. And when I woke up it was a dragon with fire in his mouth."

"Oh?" I said, half to The Boy and half to the computer screen.

"So I got out my broom-sword and I jumped on my yak."

"Your yak?"

"Yes and then we saw a hughnormous dinosaur with sharp claws like this!" I looked to see his fingers clenched into tiny pink talons. By his growl and clenched teeth I could see it was one fearsome beast. And there was no way I was getting any writing done with a monster like that in the room.

Instead I started wondering about this dragon-dinosaur fixation so many kids are consumed with. Is it their size? Is it some sort of original-sin archetypal fear of snakes? Or is it that they exist today only in books and movies?

I asked The Boy, and his answer was much more simple than I expected. He likes dinosaurs and dragons, he said, "because I want to try to defeat them."

Of course, this needed elaboration: "Fighting them and throwing stuff at them, big stones and rocks. Shoot arrows at them and poking them. Dropping arrows on their heads and pushing out their teeth. ..."

"But why do you want to defeat them?" I asked.

"Because they try to eat people — I'm the bravest dinosaur and dragon fighter in the world!"

The Boy scampered off with his broom-sword singing "Whumpity-whumpity." If what he said was true, it's not the dragons and dinosaurs that are so cool, it's the idea of defeating the dragon — of being the hero who can kill the beast.

When I was a kid it wasn't dinosaurs and dragons, it was Dracula and Frankenstein in an early-'70s monster movie comeback. Later, the beast became Darth Vader, and for my parents it was cow-rustlers and Martians. The beast changes, but what stays the same is the fantasy of being the victorious hero, who has all the traits pre-schoolers are trying to develop: They're strong, in control and, most important, brave.

We've always had a cautious kid, but as he understands more, he has more to be afraid of, and we have more to explain. Yes, the food processor chops up carrots, but it's not going to chase you screaming across the room. Yes, the rain will stop; we don't need to build an ark. No, the flying monkeys aren't real. Yes, Daddy will be back home tonight, he'd never leave you.

These are the fears of a child, fears you don't have to worry about when you're an adult, or when you're a dragon-defeater.

That explains a lot, and it tells me a lot about what's going on in my kid's life. But there's one thing still bugging me: Why is my son riding a yak?

June 5, 2001

For Richer, for Poorer, for Pudding

On Feb. 16, 1998, just past midnight, I was holding my wife up by her arms at a birth center as our son's head crowned. An hour later as he lay nursing at her breast, we looked at one another, laughing and crying and knowing God exists.

Five years and a few months earlier she surprised me in a premarital counseling session by outlining her precise plan to have a child five years after we were married, then another one four years later, then another four years after that. She had our schedule down almost to the month. My answer to the same question had been something like, "Yeah, I guess I want a coupla kids."

As I write this at 12:30 a.m. my 3-year-old son is upstairs staying awake by jabbering stories to himself and loudly singing made-up songs. His mother did the same thing as a child, only her songs were about fairy princesses instead of Batman. I went upstairs to tuck him in and tell him to go to sleep. He was sitting in the middle of a pile of books and "reading" to himself — another trait picked up from my wife, only she can actually read.

About 10 days after my son was born, he was screaming nonstop, losing weight and had a dry diaper. We realized that despite all the pumping and supplements and consultants, my wife had an insufficient milk supply and our son simply wasn't getting enough nourishment. We cried together as I gave my son his first bottle of formula.

Two-and-a-half years later we were at the dinner table choking on our food after The Boy sat up and said, "Some days it's hard. Some days it's not. Some days it's pudding."

A few months ago my wife and I got in a major argument over something insignificant that I can't remember now. She stormed out of the house to run some errands with our son. I slammed things around in the bathroom getting ready to leave for work, hoping they'd still be gone when I left so I wouldn't have to see her again that day.

Less than a week later I was hugging and kissing my wife goodbye in the kitchen on my way to work. The Boy walked up and said, "I want to hug too!" We picked him up and had a family hug, with kisses, and I felt I'd had a glimpse of heaven.

Eight years ago on this day, on June 12, 1993, I held hands with a beautiful woman in a church and we laughed when the priest said "for richer, for poorer," because we both knew the latter was more likely than the former, at least when it came to money. We were right.

Just over five years later, I was alone in my newborn son's room rocking him to sleep, bawling my eyes out as I made him a promise: "I will never leave you. Your mother and I will always be married. And I will always love her."

Our children deserve nothing less.

June 12, 2001

End in Sight for Daddy's Trash Burden

I have taken out the trash once a week ever since I was 3 years old.

I have taken out the trash 1,508 times in a row in four states.

Now, I believe, it's someone else's turn. And that's why I had a son.

One day soon my son will be big enough to sit on the front step next to a tied up trash bag, just like I did at his age, and mumble preschooler curses about how life isn't fair and someone else should have to take out the trash and nobody loves me, etc.

My mom overheard me and said my rant was something like "Darn peanut butter friggle fraggle trash."

About 10 years later I shouted profanities of a harsher sort when a full bag of ripe trash split open halfway to the bins, spilling stinky garbage all over the sidewalk.

My mom overheard those curses, too, but was once again too busy laughing at me to come up with any punishment.

I don't think The Boy is ready for that yet.

Or at least I'm not ready to wash his mouth out with soap.

So, to build up to trash duty we're starting with more simple chores: setting the table (two forks for Daddy, three spoons and maybe a plastic toy dragon for Mommy), clearing the table (don't forget to tell him NOT to throw glasses into the sink) and, of course, cleaning up his toys.

This last duty is the hardest for him, partly because he has the attention span of, well, a 3-year-old. He'll pick up a truck and stand there fiddling with the wheels for 10 minutes before remembering he was on his way to the toy box, if he remembers at all.

He has a similar distraction problem with getting dressed. He can change clothes really well, but midway through he has to run all over the house shouting "Woo-hoo! I'm naked!" I'm hoping he'll grow out of it before college.

One chore The Boy's gotten good at is feeding The Cat.

We keep a big container of dry food in the kitchen, and, when we remind him to, The Boy scoops some out and drops it all over the floor near The Cat's dish.

He gathers up the dropped pieces, along with anything else on the floor, and puts them in the food dish.

Then he calls The Cat, who never comes because he's still afraid of any person shorter than four feet, partly because they put anything they find on the floor in his food dish.

What gives me hope for the future, however, is that last week The Boy noticed The Cat's dish was empty and filled it up without being asked.

Now, I know that's just a fluke, and I can't expect him to do it every day.

But if I can keep the momentum going it may be only a matter of weeks before I can sit back, relaxing on the sofa with my newspaper and a cup of coffee, and say, "Son, take out the darn peanut butter friggle fraggle trash."

June 19, 2001

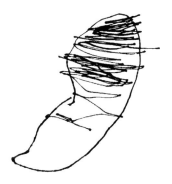

Baseball Parenting Has Dads in Pickle

For his first baseball game snack, The Boy wanted a pickle. We were at a Little League game in my hometown where my twin brothers were playing, and we'd only watched for five minutes when my son got bored.

We got up and wandered to the concession stand, where I saw pickles on the menu — one of my son's new favorites.

I ordered what I thought was going to be a few slices or a pickle spear. Nope. It was a big ol' honkin whole dill pickle. The Boy had never had one like that and I wasn't sure if he'd go for it. But what the heck, it's baseball.

We sat down in the shade behind home plate — me and my hot dog, him and his pickle — and waited for my brothers to come up at bat. Both of us almost dropped our food when a man sitting in front of us screamed, "Joey! Move closer to the plate!"

The batter looked to his coach in the dugout, who walked over and spoke some instructions into his ear. The batter replanted his feet at the plate, standing exactly where he had before.

"Fine!" the man shouted with sarcasm. "Listen to your coach, not your dad. Coach knows best." He then muttered something I wish he hadn't said in earshot of my kid.

"Hey Daddy?" The Boy said. "I think this pickle is not good."

"What's wrong with it?"

"It's wet on my fingers."

I took the aluminum foil from my hot dog, wrapped it around the bottom half of the pickle and gave it back to him.

Joey swung and missed.

"Aw! Come on, Joey! Watch the ball!" his father screamed.

Joey was either deaf or was doing his best to ignore his father.

The boy tried to take a bite of his pickle. I think the tough, rubbery skin creeped him out. "This pickle is not good," he said.

"Here, let me fix it." I took the first bite of the pickle for him, and, yes, the skin was pretty gross. I handed it back, but his mind was fixed. "I don't want it."

I considered what I'd do if I were Joey's dad.

"Aw, come on!" I'd shout, face turning red, veins popping in my neck. "That's a heckuva good pickle! Eat the pickle!" After the first bite: "You call that a bite? Choke up on that pickle, Boy!"

I wrapped up the pickle and put it away for the car trip home while The Boy ate my nacho chips.

Maybe I'm wrong. Maybe Joey will grow up to be the most well-rounded, balanced pitcher in major league baseball. And maybe I was too accommodating over the pickle. I guess I could have chided and scolded The Boy for the next five innings, making him feel worthless for not eating what he asked for. But you know what? I'd rather he remember that day as his first baseball game with Dad, not as the day Dad shoved a 50-cent pickle down his throat.

By the way, Joey drew a walk to first base, stole his way to third and got a run. He made his dad proud.

July 3, 2001

Six Rules of Life from a 3-Year-Old

My son and I recently had an in-depth conversation about discipline and what it means to be a good guy or a bad guy. The Boy came up with a list of rules that reflect all the wisdom and training his parents have instilled in him over his three years. I thought I'd share them as six life lessons we can all learn from. Maybe.

1. "Don't bring your hammer to the YMCA." The reason for this should be obvious. A 5-inch long plastic hammer can be a ruthless weapon in the hands of a preschooler. This hammer, according to The Boy, has sharp blades on the back that shoot fire. And when he walks into a room carrying the hammer, there's scary background music ("danh, dan-dah"). A weapon like that has no place in the kids' gym at the Y.

2. "Don't blow your whistle inside." The theme for The Boy's third birthday was police, so we gave each kid a party favor bag that included a whistle. After about a half-hour of shrill whistling,

the nerves of every parent were entirely shot. Oddly enough, several of the whistles were "forgotten" and left at our house. These whistles later mysteriously disappeared — all except one, and it's an "outside whistle." It's only for using outdoors because if you use it inside, monsters will come and eat your toes.

3. "Don't wiggle in your bed." This is particularly important if you've talked The Daddy into lying down to help you take a nap. If The Daddy is sleepy and really is going to take a nap, you better be still and close your eyes instead of, say, rolling over, fidgeting with the blankets, talking to your stuffed animals, picking your nose, singing, asking for water and rolling over again. If The Daddy is only pretending to sleep and is waiting for you to doze off so he can finally go to the hardware store, you need to stop keeping yourself awake by tossing around in bed. Again, monsters are waiting to eat your toes.

4. "Don't drop some big rocks in the orange sea." I have no idea what he's talking about on this one, but it looks to me like the beginnings of environmentalism. We may have a tree-hugging Greenpeace hippie on our hands.

5. "Don't throw things up in the air." For example, Matchbox cars, apple slices, Legos, cups of milk, books and, especially, hammers with sharp blades on the back that shoot fire.

6. "Naughty people must sit in the dungeon." I swear, we have never made our son sit in the dungeon. Actually, we don't even have a dungeon. We do have a scary old root cellar in the basement, and I suppose I could put a stretching table in there and a few leg irons, but somehow I don't think dungeon torture is an appropriate form of child discipline. (Don't think it hasn't crossed my mind.)

Those are the rules. I'm glad we've got that straightened out, and I hope that we can learn to abide by them, and thereby create a safer, stronger, kinder society.

As The Boy put it, "That's it; that's what all it says."

July 10, 2001

Demon Child Comes Out in Long Drive

A friend of ours whose daughter is going through the terrible twos e-mailed my wife in desperation, "Please tell me your son is sometimes the Terror Monster Demon Child."

Well, let's see.

This summer we took a trip down to Florida to visit my mom and stepdad. The Boy did well enough on the way down, and while in Florida he charmed Mimi and Papa with his best behavior. Of course it helped that he was being showered with attention.

But the trip back? Oh, the trip back.

Nine hours to go:

"Mommy I'm hungry."

"No, we just ate. I think you're bored, honey — why don't you take a nap?"

The Boy bursts into tears, crying out "I'm not sleepy!"

Eight hours to go:

"Mommy I'm thirsty."

The Mommy hands me a lidded cup with a straw and I pass it back to The Boy. "Don't drink it too fast or you'll get sick again." (Which is what he did on the way down, after chugging 16 ounces of juice in less than five minutes.)

He takes two short sips and hands it back, whining, "I don't want this."

Seven hours to go:

"I want my truck."

"How do you ask nicely?" The Mommy says.

"Please I want my truck please."

Good enough. The Mommy struggles behind her to get the truck and hands it to him.

"No," he whines. "The other truck."

"What other truck? There is no other truck," she says.

He bursts into tears.

Six hours to go:

"I'm going to throw up!"

We race to pass him a small plastic trash can. He sticks his head in, but doesn't throw up; he just makes a few spitting sounds.

Five hours to go:

He's still spitting in the trash can, trying to make himself throw up.

"You're not sick," I insist. "Hand me the trash can."

"But I'm going to throw up!"

He bursts into tears again. I've had it. I reach behind me and take away the trash can, which, of course, makes things worse.

"Remind me again why we don't beat our child?" my wife jokes, trying to keep both of us from exploding.

Four hours, 30 minutes to go:

He's still crying.

Then the idea hits me. "Boy!" I bellow. "If you don't stop whining and crying right now I will pull this car over and take off your shirt! You will have to ride without a shirt for the entire rest of the trip; do you understand?"

The Mommy grits her teeth to keep from laughing.

"Do you understand!?"

"... I understand."

He stops whining. Ten minutes later he's asleep.

I wouldn't say he's a demon child, but he is prone to possession. Lucky for me he's also afraid of losing his shirt.

July 31, 2001

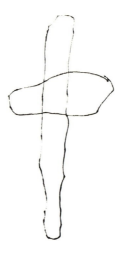

Popsicle Sticks and 'Kumbaya'

When I heard our son was old enough for vacation Bible school this year, I was excited. Just like his good ol' dad, he'd learn to sing "Kumbaya" and make practical objects out of popsicle sticks.

It would be hosted by our church's neighboring Presbyterians, so we knew he wouldn't be learning goat sacrifice or handling of poisonous chickens.

But The Mommy wasn't so thrilled. It's not that she doesn't like practical objects made out of popsicle sticks, or that she's afraid of Presbyterians. It's that we've never left The Boy for that much time with anyone other than our parents or a trusted, well-known babysitter.

What if he started crying? (Someone would pick him up.) What if there were an accident? (Someone would call us.) What if Presbyterians really DO handle poisonous chickens? (The Boy would tell them "No, no!")

Of course The Boy was excited about the whole thing, even

more so when we arrived and he saw his friend "Revurnd Gracey" wearing a makeshift police officer's cap standing in the street directing traffic. And it turned out several of his younger friends were there, too. We dropped him off with his name tag in his assigned row, then lingered a bit at the back of the church, mulling over second thoughts about leaving him.

The Boy didn't care. He was staring, entranced, at a puppet show. No chickens.

As we drove off, we turned on a talk radio station to keep us from thinking. Once home, the door closed behind me and I felt a sudden jolt of panic: "Where's The Boy — who's watching The Boy?" I told myself he's with people who know him and know us. He's fine. He loves stuff like this. But in my mind I pictured myself telling the police I'd last seen my son listening to a zebra puppet talk about God.

Three hours later we picked him up. And, as we feared, he'd been crying. He said he was "being cranky." But he was excited about showing us what he'd made: a paper star glued to, yes, a popsicle stick.

The next day The Boy was a little less "cranky," and made a bird feeder on yet another popsicle stick. By Day 3 he was really into it. On the way home he talked about having a cookout with his friends and coloring and singing songs. Plus he'd made his best project yet: A rock with paper glued to it and some heart stickers. That will still be on prominent display in the bookshelf when he's ready for college, whether he likes it or not.

By the end of the week we were much more relaxed ("The Boy? What Boy?"). And The Boy learned a song: "Love the Lord your God with all of your heart, with all of your soul, with all of your strength, with all of your mind and your neighbor as yourself." When you say "soul" you point to your feet.

A song like that's worth finding places for practical objects made with popsicle sticks. And it's worth us feeling a bit panicky. The world would be a heckuva lot better if every kid knew a song like that.

Now if we can only work in the word "Kumbaya" ...

August 7, 2001

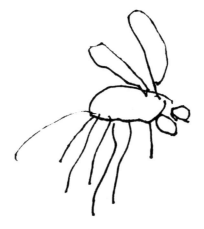

Kid Motto: 'Born to Be Rude'

The Boy had spent the afternoon at Nana and Grandaddy's, and when we arrived to pick him up he had all sorts of stories to tell of what he'd done while we were gone. He led me to the front porch and showed me a pile of dead bugs.

"These damosquitoes were after me and Grandaddy, and trying to bite us ..."

"These what?"

"Damosquitoes. And Grand-daddy gave them a smack!"

"Um, let's not call them 'damosquitoes.' Let's call them 'bad mosquitoes' instead."

"OK."

Now if I were a truly strict parent, I guess I'd wash his mouth out with anti-bacterial soap. But he was only repeating what Grandaddy said, and obviously the soap never worked on him. Plus, after three years of this, I'm starting to think that kids, while they may not be born evil, are born terribly rude. A lot of my parenting lately seems to be a cycle of him doing rude things and me telling him not to do them again.

We had some friends over for dinner, one of whom was a priest. The Boy came in and sat for a while on the couch. Then, without comment, The Boy leaned over the back of the couch, spat on the floor and sat back down again to listen to more of the conversation. My instinct was to yell at him, but I stopped myself when I realized that, come to think of it, we'd never actually told him not to spit on the floor. Of course, he'd never done this before, and must've decided that since there was a priest in the room that would be a good time to try it out — if we beat him to death he could at least get last rites.

The Mommy had more composure. She said "Excuse me" and walked The Boy into the kitchen, where she explained to him that we do not spit on the floor. "Oh! OK." She gave him a rag and had him go clean it up.

Saying "excuse me" is something he's gotten really good at. We taught him that so he wouldn't be so rude in interrupting conversations. Of course, he still interrupts, but now it has a polite ring to it. As soon as The Mommy asks me, "So how was your day?" The Boy walks up and repeats "Excuse me" until we let him tell us a stream-of-consciousness story about pirates or superheroes. We're working on that one.

Sometimes I think maybe we're expecting too much — being too strict. There is the alternative of letting him do whatever he wants and figure it out on his own. But a bit of wisdom came to me recently in Disney's "Peter Pan." The Lost Boys wear animal skins and do nothing but fight, scrap, cuss and yell, all because they don't have parents telling them how to behave politely, which, it turns out, is something they're actually yearning for.

It comes down to this: I could risk being too strict and having my kid mad at me for the next 15 years. Or I could risk raising a kid who dresses up like a badger, spits on the floor, interrupts people and identifies things as "damosquitoes," "dampoliticians" and "damnewspapers." I think I'll risk being too strict.

August 21, 2001

'Gerjus Kur' Takes Detour in Learning

"Daddy, here's a kurter fur de pur."

"A what?" The Boy had run into the bathroom with his Robin Hood mask on and was handing me a penny.

"A kurter fur de pur. Ta feed de pur people."

"Oh! You mean 'a quarter for the poor.'"

"Yeah, a kurterfurdepur." He gallumphed off on his make-believe horse to find another penny.

I'm enjoying this pronunciation problem while it lasts, and I'm doing my best not to make fun of him. He's never made the "th" sound, always substituting "d" (this, that, those becomes dis, dat, doze), and now The Boy's problem with "or" is becoming clear. We discovered it during a car ride as he was telling us how he killed a dragon with his sword.

"Say 'sword' again?"

"Surd!"

"Say 'board.'"

"Burd!"
"Say 'gorgeous.'"
"Gurjus!"
"Say 'or.'"
"Ur!"

We had to stop. We were laughing so hard The Boy was starting to wonder what was so funny.

I'm torn between correcting his speech or letting him figure it out on his own. He used to have a problem with "f," saying "schive shrogs" instead of "five frogs," and calling our neighbor "Sank" instead of "Frank." We taught him how to pronounce his f's, because that was actually getting hard to understand.

"Hey Boy. Say 'fah.'"
"Fah!"
"Say 'rog.'"
"Rog!"
"Fah-rog."
"Fah-rog!"
"Frog."
"Schrog!"

A week or so of that and he was over the "f" problem. But I'm not so sure I should keep correcting him on "or" and "d" and whatever else comes next. On the one hand, I don't want to give him a complex about how he talks, but I also don't want him to still be saying "Jurj" instead of "George" when he's in college. That sort of thing can actually be dangerous. When I was in high school, I got punched several times for calling the local bully "Gery" instead of "Gary," and I still have trouble pronouncing it the right way.

The other vocal quirk The Boy's picked up is stammering. I guess his thoughts are racing faster than he can express them and he gets caught on a word, usually "and, and, and" or "but, but, but." I've found the trick is to be patient and keep listening while he finishes. Of course, that's easier said than done, but the patience always pays off. For example, when we get to hear jokes like this:

"Hey Daddy? Why did Scharmer Scham grow kurn nex to his burn?"

"I don't know, Boy. Why did Farmer Sam grow corn next to his barn?"

"Becuz becuz becuz becuz becuz becuz becuz becuz his kur was on schire!"

Hah! ... What? You don't get it?

For now I suppose we'll be patient and let him figure it out. It may be that for a year or so, The Mommy and I will be the only ones who understand everything he says. And I suppose that if anyone needs me to translate, I can do that too — but it might cost you a kurter.

August 28, 2001

Good Dads Chase Rabbits in Pajamas

I am no longer cool.
Not that I've ever been particularly cool to begin with, but something about having a kid has turned me into the biggest dork on the planet. And it seems like lately the world is conspiring to prove just how big of a dork I am.

A friend and I got in a conversation at work that led me to mention how much I enjoy the humor snippets in "Reader's Digest." "You read 'Reader's Digest?'" she asked. Yes, I told her, we've had a subscription for years. She tumbled out laughing. I immediately protested I've been reading some highbrow novels, too: Maughm, Pynchon and Solzhenitsyn. I didn't mention, however, how often I get a kick out of The Boy's subscription to "Highlights" magazine.

Also at work, we were discussing in a news meeting a story about the dance-club drug Ecstasy, and someone asked, sarcastically, what I knew about dance clubs. I started to say I used to go clubbing all the time, back before I had a kid, but the laughter in the room drowned me out.

Then there was the day I went out to my front steps to clip my fingernails (a cool thing to do, right?) and was in the process of covering my arms and legs in bug spray when I saw two young women walking down the street toward me. One of them, I thought, was The Boy's baby sitter. I shouted "Afternoon ladies!" and waved to them, then sat down to start clipping. As the girls got closer, I heard one of them say, disdainfully, "Who's THAT?" I looked up and realized it wasn't my son's baby sitter after all — just two teenage girls walking down the street staring at the doofus weirdo on his front steps clipping his nails.

The final straw for me was the morning when The Boy and The Mommy saw from the bedroom window a rabbit eating lettuce in our garden. I jumped into action and ran out the door, wearing only my pajamas, with The Boy's toy shield on one arm and with the other swinging his broom-sword above my head. I galloped across the yard shouting a battle cry at the fleeing rabbit . . . just as my next-door neighbors rolled down the driveway. I walked back up the driveway, suddenly remembering I was still in pajamas. "Uh, hey Chris," they said.

"I'm chasing rabbits," I said.

"Oh."

Somehow, maybe to make me look even dorkier, The Mommy is still hip. Last week she taught about 20 people how to tie-dye shirts — including me. At least I can say I hang out with cool people.

Of course, to The Boy I am cool. Who else would rescue Mommy's garden from rabbits AND read "Highlights" magazine to him? Who else can give him piggy-back rides across the library parking lot, whittle sticks into arrows and play giant-attacks-the-pirate-ship? None of this is particularly cool, unless you're 3 years old. But I've had my chance to be cool, and now's my chance to be a daddy. As long as I'm cool to him, I guess I don't mind if I'm a big doofus to everyone else.

September 4, 2001

Tough Editor in a Small Package

Over breakfast, The Mommy was enjoying the newspaper, and I noticed she was looking at a page a designer and I had wrestled with the night before.

"Do you know what a pain in the butt it was to put that page together?" I commented.

"Daddy!" The Boy said. "That's bathroom talk!"

"It is?" I said.

"Yes. You can only talk about that in the bathroom."

"OK," I said, reaching for a notebook to write down another idea for a column.

"Are you going to write a dad column?"

"Maybe," I said.

"You have to do a dad column about me and you and Mommy doing a family hug."

"I do?" I asked. "Why?"

"Because it's fun. Because I love all your heart and your self."

Yes, he's definitely his mother's son — mushy from the start. I changed the subject. "Hey, Boy, what is a dad column, anyway?"

"It's about the things what you do and not do."

That's actually as good a definition of a column as I've ever heard. "I think I should do a dad column about you being a superhero."

"I am a superhero," he said.

"I know. What makes you a superhero?"

"Because I have pixie dust and a wing."

For the uninitiated, "pixie dust" is the stuff that comes out of Tinkerbell when Peter Pan shakes her. If you get covered in pixie dust, you can fly (You can fly! You can fly!!). A "wing" is a cape. One day in church our priest turned around quickly, causing his robes to billow. The Boy gasped and said, "Does he have a wing?" When I said, "Yeah, sort of," he asked, "Can he fly?"

But back to our conversation. "What else makes you a superhero?"

"I fight bad guys with gas." (He ain't kidding — the kid loves broccoli.) "Gasoline powers my electricity."

"It does? Well why do you need electricity?"

"That's how my superhero power works. It goes all through my leggage."

"Your leggage?"

"Yeah, and inside me is a big hughnormous rock from our planet."

"What planet is that?"

"Africa."

That was it. That was enough. I downed my coffee and went to the computer to start writing my next column. I got about 10 minutes of writing in before I heard the drumming of 6-inch feet across the kitchen floor and into the den.

"Daddy? What are you doing?"

"Writing."

"Let's play pirates."

"In a little while ..." I muttered, not really paying attention.

He wandered off. I felt guilty and a bit hypocritical. Here I was writing a column about fatherhood while ignoring my son. But with 3-year-olds there are plenty of second chances. And sure enough, about 10 minutes later he was back, and he was indignant.

"Look, that's enough writing I told you!"

All right, all right. But just for that, someone's getting turned upside down and tickled.

October 2, 2001

Costumed Daddy a Treat for Little Ghouls

We didn't really need to ask The Boy what he wanted to be for Halloween last year. After I explained a bit about costumes and trick-or-treating, I offered a few suggestions, and he jumped at the one I knew would bring him on board: policeman.

And since The Boy was a policeman, The Mommy and I dressed as bad guys, complete with masks and plastic handcuffs. I felt a bit ridiculous. But I had inspiration from the man who taught me the true spirit of Halloween: my stepfather.

As excited as The Boy is to be a policeman, he's outdone by my stepfather, who actually is a cop. He's a real one with a patrol car, a siren and a radio. When my stepfather got word of the costume idea, he started asking for pictures. It didn't matter that Halloween was a month off, he wanted The Boy in the costume right then.

My stepfather's always been a sucker for Halloween. One year my mom came home from work and half-glanced at him on the porch. As she juggled her things and walked up the steps, she told him about her day and her drive home, etc. Then she looked over and screamed.

It wasn't my stepfather on the porch. It was a headless dummy he'd made by stuffing some old clothes with rags — some of them red to look like blood.

Every year Mom complains about the talking skulls he sets up all over the house that shout stupid puns when you walk by, like "Watch your head" and "I've got my eyes on you."

But the best part about Halloween with him was trick-or-treating. Rather than sending us off on our own, my stepfather put on this old, stinky orange wig and went door-to-door with us. He'd follow us for hours, watching out for us and the other kids in the neighborhood.

I always thought he was being a typical paranoid cop. He'd seen what real bad guys are like and was probably nervous as a black cat to have us out knocking on strangers' doors. But what I like about it is he didn't walk around with his hands in his pockets giving people dirty looks. With that stinky orange wig he looked ridiculous, and at 11 years old that's exactly what I needed to see: My normally stern and strict stepfather making a fool of himself with us kids.

I think all kids need to see dad being silly. That's why this year, if I can ever get organized enough to work out the details, I'll be in costume again. The Boy wants to be a knight, so of course The Mommy will be a princess, and me? I'm a dragon. I'll be walking around our neighborhood in green pajamas with a bunch of children. I'll do it because I know my son is gallumphing along next to me on an imaginary horse, and he needs somebody to defeat with his "serd."

I'll do it because my kid needs to see me having fun more than I need to worry about looking foolish.

Besides, I kinda like trick-or-treating, and there's a good chance I might get a Reese's cup out of this.

October 30, 2001

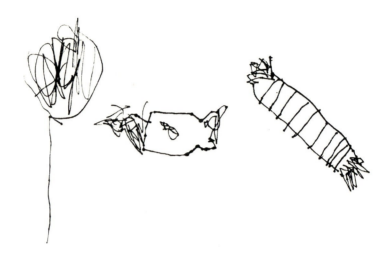

Smart Dads Keep Quiet About Treats

Have you finished your Halloween candy?

Are you working your way to the best pieces, getting those daily sugar highs, experimenting with combos of caramel and bubble gum?

Or did you eat it all in one fell swoop and moan like a dying walrus the next day?

No, kids, I'm not talking to you; I'm talking to your dads. You guys know what I mean: The kids are finally asleep, Mommy's reading in the living room, and on your way back from the loo you stop by the kitchen to grab a handful from the big plastic jack-o'-lantern on top of the fridge. Mmm. Sweet Tarts.

Last year this was so easy we didn't have to hide the candy. The Boy was only 2 and didn't care much for sweets. While he munched on some carrots or cheese, I'd schnarf down bags of M&Ms straight from his pumpkin.

This year I figured he'd still be a health nut. During trick-or-treating, one of my neighbors tried to tease The Boy by offering bags of frozen vegetables. "Green beans or black-eyed peas?" he said. The Boy excitedly shot back, "Black-eyed peas!"

Oh yeah, I thought, that candy's all mine.

We got back to the house and spread out his loot on the table, then divided it up according to the four basic food groups: hard candy, chocolates, powders and gum. I laid claim to 50 percent of the Reese's cups, and The Mommy took her share of powders. The Boy was fine with this blatant candy theft. In fact, he was already digging into his favorite: the popcorn.

Later that night I wanted to see how The Boy reacted to various candies, such as the sour Shock Tarts (his face crinkled up, but he ate it). Then I made my fatal error. I encouraged him to try a Reese's Cup. "I like that very much!" he said. For the rest of the night we tried all the best candy in the basket.

As we munched away The Mommy chatted on the phone with a friend from college.

"What are you up to? ... Oh, I'm just I'm watching my husband eat all of my child's Halloween candy."

The Boy heard this and looked at me. I gave myself away by laughing, which prompted him to pick up his pumpkin basket and carry it behind the sofa.

"I'm going to put this where it will be safe," he said, hiding the basket in his toy box.

"Safe from who?" I asked.

"From bad guys."

That may have been my son's first blatant lie, or maybe not.

But he still had a pile of Skittles, and I asked if I could have a few.

"No," he said cautiously.

"You don't want to share them?"

"Daddy, I don't want to talk about this."

So now the truth is out. My son knows I'm a candy thief, and becoming a daddy hasn't changed that - it's only lowered the age of my victims. Next year, when The Baby's here, The Boy should breathe a bit easier. His loot will be safe. I'll take the new little one with us, and getting sweets from her will be like taking candy from a ... oh ... well, never mind.

November 13, 2001

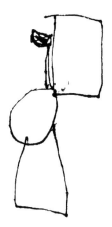

Why You Should 'Go' Before You Leave

Overheard all across America, just as the men's room door swings open:

"I thought you went to the potty before we left."

"I did go potty but nothing came out. It was all empty."

"OK. Now remember: Don't touch anything."

"OK. Hey Daddy? I need to go poop too."

"Oh Lord. Well, we're not using that stall."

"Why?"

"It's gross. Somebody made a mess."

"Why did somebody make a mess?"

"Because some people were never taught by their daddies to act right. And they have bad aim. This stall is OK. Stop! Don't touch that!"

"Why?"

"Because I SAID so."

"... But is there a reason?"

"... Yes, it's dirty. There, I've wiped it off, now pull down your pants and I'll hold you up here."

"Don't let me fall in."

"I would NEVER let you fall in."

"Why don't they have any little boy potties?"

"Because whoever designed this bathroom doesn't have children."

"Hey, there's somebody next door! I see his feet. Hello?"

"Shh. He's busy. Leave him be."

"Is he going potty too?"

"He needs privacy. Let's discuss something else."

"Why is this a potty?"

"... What?"

"Why is this a potty?"

"... Because it is. Do you mean 'How do we know it's a potty?'"

"No, I mean 'Why is this a potty?'"

"... Are you done?"

"Yeah. That was hard work."

"OK, shake. ... Good job. OK, I'll do that. ... There you go. DON'T TOUCH THE POTTY!"

"Sorry."

"Now stand right there and wait for Daddy."

"La, la, la, my bottom went to the potty."

"Boy, stop singing that. That's bathroom talk."

"But we're in the bathroom."

"... Good point."

"La, la la, my bottom ..."

"OK, you're singing right in my ear. Can you whisper instead?"

"OK, I'll just open the door."

"Don't touch the door! Put your hands in your pockets, stand still, and be quiet for 15 seconds."

"... How long is 15 seconds?"

"That wasn't it. OK, back up."

"Can I flush it?"

"It flushes by itself."

"Is it magic?"

"Sure is. Now, move over so I can open the door. All right, let's wash our hands."

"I can't reach!"

"Wait, I'll pick you up."

"Why isn't there a stool?"

"Because whoever designed this bathroom doesn't have children."

"Why don't they have children?"

"Because all they ever do is design bathrooms."

"Why do I have to wash my hands?"

"So you don't infect Middle Tennessee with cholera."

"Huh?"

"Because Daddy says so. OK hold your hands under the blower and rub them together. ... OK now put your head under the blower. ... Now you look silly. Let's go."

"Can I open the door?"

"Uh, why don't you let me get it."

"Thanks Dad."

December 4, 2001

Family Tradition Has Way of Making Itself

I've been looking forward to this Christmas since The Boy was born. This would be the Christmas he's 3 1/2. This Christmas he'd join in the great family tradition of putting together the artificial tree. We'd have happy family pictures in our Christmas sweaters, handing one another branches, straight out of Norman Rockwell — well, kinda.

I'm a sucker for Christmas, and with everybody from Frank Capra to Bing Crosby on my side, I don't have a hard time getting a mental image of what Christmas should be. I've got a growing family to complete the picture, so how could Christmas come out as anything other than the perfect holiday like the still-frame in my head?

Easy.

The sweater was the first thing to go — I broke a sweat five minutes into unpacking the tree. Next was my patience. I ought to know by now that "wait" doesn't register with 3-year-olds. And there's no way to put a tree together when a preschooler is jabbing you with metal branches. After getting bored watching me work, The Boy wandered off to play. And that was fine, because frankly, he was driving me nuts. So much for Norman Rockwell.

Once the tree was up, The Mommy brought The Boy back in, along with some hot mugs of spiced tea, and opened the ornament boxes. The Boy's job was to find places for the 12 wooden apples. He did — all bunched together on the same branch. Oh well.

Next was the big moment: Putting the angel on top. Not since Yukon Cornelius brought back the Bumble would there be a star-raising this meaningful. I gave The Boy the angel and put him on my shoulders. He reached. I stretched. No good. The tip of the tree was just out of reach. So I did it myself. Forget Norman Rockwell, this wasn't even Charlie Brown.

The only thing left was the tinsel, which The Boy dumped in the tree by the handful, leaving wadded clumps all over the lower branches.

Once done, we dimmed the lights and sat down to admire our work, such as it was, and I told myself I'll just have to wait until next year — when The Boy's older and better able to help me — before I can enjoy family Christmas traditions.

As The Mommy and I finished our drinks, The Boy came in with a chiffon scarf, which he held in front of his face so he could look through it at the tree. It was ridiculous, but he went on so much about how cool it looked, we had to see for ourselves. He was right — the scarf filtered out all the wires and ornaments, making the tree a wavy silhouette. All we could see were the lights, with a tiny rainbow around each one.

I looked at the tree without the scarf, and The Boy's small grove of packed apple ornaments. These aren't the traditions I'd planned for, but who am I to say what Christmas should be? Christmas is Christmas, and part of the fun is not knowing what's in that stocking. It might be George Bailey, it might be Charlie Brown, or it might be a little boy making his own traditions with a chiffon scarf and a clumpy handful of tinsel.

December 11, 2001

New Year's Resolutions For Dads

All right, women, stop reading this. This is top-secret guy stuff, and if we told you about it, we'd have to kill you. Or at least subject you to loud belching.

Guys, what we need is some good New Year's resolutions. We all want to enjoy our wives and our kids more, and the best way to do that is to get organized. I've got some thoughts on that, so bear with me and see if these resolutions work under your roof.

1. I will, at least once a day, look my kid in the eyes and listen to what he's telling me. Even if it's "Lasterday, when the monster was in the prayloom, by the chair where Mommy sits, when she's reading her book, about all the cool things, and there's no pictures, but she likes there's no pictures ..." I will listen. Without interrupting or laughing.

2. I will, at least once a month, do something especially kind

or romantic for my wife. Guys, there's no arguing with research, and research tells us families don't work unless moms and dads are happy. So make your wife happy. You may not care so much about a flower, an "I love you," or a surprise cleaning of the toilets, but for her you might go from the dud behind the remote control to the studly romantic hero, and there's nothing wrong with that.

3. I will not wear black socks with shorts while mowing the lawn until I have grandchildren. Look, guys, I know you're sometimes tempted, but the whole black socks and sneakers deal is a fashion luxury reserved for the granddads. No skipping your place in line, making the rest of us look bad.

4. I will put a note on my dresser that says, "The whole point of work is to support my family, not the other way around." That's a hard one for a lot of us. But think about it, which would make your hands quiver more: a pink slip or divorce papers? Work's important, sure, but it isn't family, and work won't be at your bedside 50 years from now when you're dying in a nursing home, wearing black socks and sneakers.

5. I will at least pretend to lower the toilet seat when I'm done.

6. I will give in to daddyhood. My favorite letter from a reader was sent by a retired Air Force colonel who, back in his daddy days, was getting ready for a black-tie formal and made the mistake of putting on a white dinner jacket before changing his newborn's diaper. There was, well, an explosive incident, and he had to find a sportscoat to wear to the party. The thing is, he pleaded that I not give his name if I used that story. In the macho world of the military, he felt he had to hide that he was a good dad. Guys, we all change diapers. We all kiss boo-boos. Being a good father to your child makes you more of a man, not less.

7. In the company of women, I will say "Excuse me" after I belch, rather than "Whew, that was a good 'un," unless, of course, the belching is to punish a woman who has read these secret resolutions, in which case no apologies are necessary.

January 1, 2002

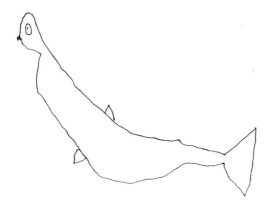

Lousy Name Part of Job for Top Toys

A plastic truck with sharp edges. A toy farmer with a yellow hat. A weird, raccoon-looking, nocturnal tree mammal. What do these have in common? Each has served time as The Boy's attachment toy — a plaything dragged everywhere and subjected to all sorts of abuse in the name of love. Kind of like Tina Turner, only made in China.

Normal kids have velveteen rabbits or teddy bears in overalls. But The Boy? His current pal is a 2-inch plastic sea lion, painted green and pale yellow, which he carries around, soliciting commentary on what the sea lion would like to do, where it would like to go and whether it might like something to eat — perhaps some tiny plastic herring. "Erm yesh," the sea lion replies. "That rould be fine."

This I might have expected. What I didn't expect was the sea lion's name: Hatch Serious.

The Boy has never been this inventive in naming things. That weird, raccoon-looking, nocturnal tree mammal was Sugar Baby. This creature exists in the wild and it's called, no kidding, a sugar baby. But most folks don't know this, and the common response when people saw Sugar Baby was "What's that? A possum?" The Boy's response: "No, it's Sugar Baby."

"But what is Sugar Baby?"

"Just Sugar Baby."

We were glad when the title of top toy passed from Sugar Baby to something more normal: a brown monkey puppet. I hoped for a good name to kick in as well, something like Fuzzytail, Oopie or Peter Tork. Nope.

"Oh, I like your monkey! What's its name?"

"Monkey."

"Yes, but what's your monkey's name?"

The Boy's brow would crunch into a furrow, as if to ask "What? Am I not speaking English here?" He'd pop back sternly, "It's just Monkey."

We thought we had a breakthrough when a friend loaned The Boy some small plastic knights, most of which look alike. The Boy took to naming them: Ax Knight, Mace Knight, Torch Knight, etc. But then, the last knight to be named got a doozy: Arrowhelmet Huzaguza. The surname was gibberish, and I loved it. I wondered, though, what was behind "Arrowhelmet." I puzzled on this a couple of days until finally I picked up Sir Huzaguza and noticed that molded on the center of his helmet is a tiny arrow, put there by Fisher-Price just to give my kid a nonoriginal name to land on.

Which brings us back to the first truly original name: Hatch Serious.

My theory on "Serious" is that The Boy was trying to remember what the animal was called. He had a walrus the same size and knew what that was. In trying to come up with "sea lion," he combined it with "walrus" to get "sea-rus," which became "Serious."

But since I wasn't sure, I asked The Boy, and here's his explanation. Hatch Serious is called "Hatch" because he has too many eggs in his house and has to come in through a hatch in the roof. He's called "Serious" because he used to be a superhero, but changed his name so the bad guys wouldn't know who he was. You see, an old pirate with only one eye had sent his crocodiles to eat this great and powerful sea lion, formerly known as ... Superhatch.

Now that's a good name.

January 22, 2002

Lingerie Mag a Major Find for a Little Boy

No one's quite sure how my in-laws started getting Victoria's Secret catalogs. They just showed up one day, and, my father-in-law — being a wise man — hasn't raised objections. Like all the other catalogs, they sit around for a few weeks, maybe serving a short term as a coaster for a hot cup of tea.

One of these lingerie catalogs was in a stack of magazines on an ottoman in my in-laws' living room last week. I'm sure The Boy was bored listening to the grown-ups, so he flipped through the stack, looking for something interesting.

And man, did he find it.

I was at work, but The Mommy told me he glanced around at the grown-ups, then ran out of the room, catalog in hand. The Mommy didn't know what he had or why he'd run out. So once she finished whatever she was saying, she called out sweetly, "Hey Boy, what are you doing?"

He said nothing, just tossed the Victoria's Secret catalog out a bedroom door, pretending he'd never seen it.

Now, there are a variety of ways to handle a situation like that.

The first one assumes the only thing more evil than being a scantily clad lady is looking at a scantily clad lady. You give the kid 10 lashes with a belt, then make him pray for his soul while burning the Victoria's Secret catalog on the grill around back of the barn. My theory is that's a great way to raise a serial killer.

The next option would be to sit down with the child and go through the catalog with him, deciding whether Raquel or Jasmine has the best thighs and trying to figure out which of the eight models DIDN'T have silicone implants. This is how you create beauty pageant judges and plastic surgeons.

Another option I learned from my mom, only I was about 14 instead of 4, and the magazine she found was not Victoria's Secret. In fact, there was nothing secret in that magazine at all. She left it up to me whether to throw it away, but she and I had a long talk about the women in the pictures. We speculated about why they took a job posing for a magazine like that, and what else they might have become if someone had showed them some respect. Since then I've never even been able to enjoy a meal at Hooters.

The Mommy and the in-laws didn't take any of these options. Instead, they carefully selected the course they felt would be best: They laughed their heads off, then called me to share the story.

I got on the phone with The Boy and asked if that was a cool catalog and were they being mean to him. He didn't want to talk about it.

The Mommy, seeing he might be confused and embarrassed, told him he could go look at the Victoria's Secret catalog if he wanted to and assured him there was nothing wrong with it. So he picked it up again and walked off. Granddaddy — being a wise man — hollered after him, "Don't go far; it's my turn to look at it when you're done!"

I'm not worried about him becoming serial killer, but I think this is how you create a fine arts student.

February 19, 2002

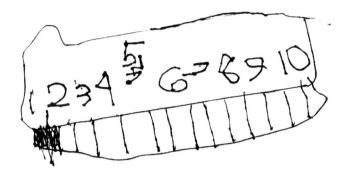

Life of Blues Starts with First 'Harlomica'

For those of you who don't know this yet, let me be clear: I'm in a mixed marriage. That's right, my wife is musically inclined, with skills on the piano and flute and a rich, beautiful voice. But me? I'm tone deaf as a socket wrench, and with about as much musical skill.

With such an extreme genetic background, we're not sure how The Boy will come out. Early signs are that he enjoys good music. When we're driving around, he prefers NPR's classical stuff and even jazz to the rock and dance stations The Daddy wants to listen to.

So last week we took the first big step in his long walk to the London Symphony Orchestra: We got him a harmonica.

We didn't actually set out for a harmonica. The plan was to buy him a drum for his fourth birthday so he could, for example, keep time for any Vikings rowing a nearby boat and lead a few troops of soldiers into battle. But the toy store didn't have a drum — not a real one anyway — so we settled for an on-sale music set that had a tambourine, maracas and, just for kicks, a harmonica.

"What's that, Daddy?"

"That? That's a harmonica."

"A harlomica. Cool."

"Harmonica. You blow in it."

He did, then looked at me like he'd just been handed fire by Prometheus, or figured out the answer on "Blues Clues."

"And you know what's really neat? When you're done, you can put it in your shirt pocket."

That was it. He's hooked. For days now we've been treated to harmonica songs, most ... well ... all of them The Boy's own compositions. There's "Hurry Hurry Home (Mouse)," which is about a mouse being chased by a tiger. There's "Sat Before the King," a total ripoff of the sixpence rhyme. "Business, Business, Business, Business" is a blues song about a job; I think that one's about me. The song dedicated to The Mommy is called "Time to Scrapbook."

He can play loud, and he can play soft (soft is preferable when The Mommy is on the phone or watching TV). He can play fast real well, but slow he's still learning. He can also not play at all, for example at the dinner table, riding in the car or when waiting for Daddy to wake up in the morning. He's still learning that, too.

Weird thing is, I've walked in the playroom a couple of times now to find him playing the harmonica, leaning on the couch like an old black man on a rust-eaten pickup by the side of some vacant Mississippi crossroads. I thought I was imagining that he was playing the blues. I mean, no one has even told him what the blues are, if such things can be told. But the other day at dinner, he said it all.

"Sometimes I play sad songs on my harlomica."

"Harmonica. You do?"

"Yeah. Sometimes when I want to play with Mommy and Daddy, and Mommy and Daddy are too busy to play with me, I play songs on my harlomica that are sad songs."

Y'know, I was hoping for a chair in the London Symphony Orchestra. But if this love affair with the harmonica lasts, I just might get a barstool on Beale Street.

February 26, 2002

Birth Coach Feels Rusty but Ready

To see childbirth on TV, you'd think it was some sort of pagan torture scene — a half-crazed woman lying on her back, screaming while an annoying bystander calmly repeats "Relax, remember to breathe." At some point the bystander is yanked to the bed by one ear and punched.

Now, I won't dispute that some births are like that. But it hasn't been our experience. The Mommy and I use the Bradley method, which relies on the husband coaching the mommy through labor, easing her pain with massage, position changes and relaxation tricks. Knocking her out with a large rubber mallet is also an option, but we haven't tried it yet.

For these methods to work, of course, you've got to know them, and The Mommy and I haven't done this in, oh, four years. A couple of weeks ago we had our first practice.

We started with massage. While watching the clock, I rubbed The Mommy's back and talked her through the timing of a contraction. Once we were done I got my first critique.

"You need to slow down with the massage. You sped up so much you were stressing me out. It's not a race, OK?"

She was right: Watching the clock put me in deadline mode, and the closer we were to the contraction being over, the faster I talked and the faster I moved, just like I do when we're trying to get the paper off the floor.

Next I tried taking her through a breathing exercise, forgetting that these don't work because of her asthma. And I forgot that she doesn't need me to tell her how bad her pain is, and that I don't need to keep babbling in her ear.

Finally we tried visualization. I described her walking on the hot sand out to the cold water, the foamy waves tickling her feet, then washing over her legs. She wades out farther and the waves push her in and out. Finally she's carried out, touching lightly with her toes the sandy floor of the ocean.

No good.

"First of all, a contraction lasts about a minute, so you're going to have to get me in the water a lot faster than that. The water should be warm, not cold. And don't have me touching the sand; I need to be floating."

I did a visualization of my own: She's floating on her back, perfectly relaxed, when a 12-pound seagull flies over and poops on her head. That relaxed me a lot.

We're rusty on the techniques, and maybe that should have me worried. But it doesn't. With the last birth, we held hands tightly; we worked as a team. This time, though, we're not just holding hands, we're two sides of the same hand. I know she can do this, and she trusts me being with her every step. We weren't as sure of these things four years ago, when we were in unknown waters and didn't know whether any 12-pound seagulls were nearby.

It's still just us, even with The Boy yelling into the kitchen, "Too much hugging and kissing!" Together we'll work out the tricks and techniques, but the most vital technique is one we've practiced all along: being together.

March 5, 2002

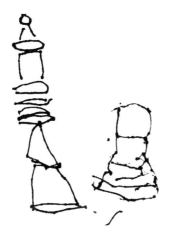

Four-Year-Old Checks the Game of Kings

It was the first good game of chess I'd had in years. We were in the home of friends, drinking big goblets of red wine and playing chess on a wooden coffee table board. We were so intent on the game we didn't notice The Boy walk up.

He must've thought we were building a castle. Castles are built so giants can knock them down.

I yelled "No!" and my opponent yelled something like "Gggnah!" Too late. We stared at the empty board for a good 10 seconds after the last piece rattled off onto the floor.

That was The Boy's first lesson in chess: Don't knock all the pieces off the board.

The next day I decided The Boy needed a few more lessons, so I rummaged in the closet, found an old chess board and sat him down for what proved to be a long afternoon of explanations.

Lesson No. 2: Pawns got a raw deal.

"Why can't my pawn go backwards?" he asked.

"Because he has to do what the king says."

"Why won't the king let the pawns go backwards?"

"Because he wants them to go fight," I said.

"Why does the king want them to go fight?"

"Because his feelings of inadequacy compel him to control the lives and deaths of his subjects. Let's talk about the queen."

Lesson No. 3: The Queen's got it made.

"She can pretty much do anything she wants," I said. "Kinda like Mommy."

"Can she go this way?"

"Well, actually no," I said. "She has to stay in a straight line."

"Kinda like Mommy?"

"... Huh?"

Lesson No. 4: Take turns.

"Move your rook here, then you can get my knight here."

"OK." The Boy moved his rook, then took the knight. "Pow!"

"No, put the rook back," I said. "You have to wait until it's your turn again to get my knight."

"But you might move your knight."

"Well, maybe I won't notice."

The Boy taught me a lot about how chess ought to be played, and now we go by some modified rules.

Boy's Rule No. 1: Don't capture the "special" knight.

"Ha! Got your knight!"

"No!" he shouted in a panic. "That's my special knight!"

"How about you swap knights, then, so your special knight can stay on the board?"

"OK." He clutched it to his chest and gave it a kiss. "Poor knighty."

Boy's Rule No. 2: Lego figures can play, too.

"What are you doing?"

"I'm making my Lego knight my chess knight," he said.

"But he won't match your other one."

"Well, I can use two Lego knights," he said.

"OK. ... Can I have one too?"

Boy's Rule No. 3: Sound effects are required.

Pawns moving forward: "Ffft."

Queen moving across board: "Rrreaww!"

King backing up: "Beep. Beep. Beep."

Anyone being captured: "Pow!" Followed by "Ugh! Agh. You got me. ... kahh."

Next time we play we might add fake blood and battle scars. Who says chess is boring?

March 12, 2002

Little Mr. Fixit Needs Work on His Solutions

Back when our house was built, somebody ran a drainpipe from our washing machine to the back yard. Now there are all sorts of environmental problems with that — not to mention having some reeking dirty socks fertilize the tulips — but a bigger problem was that the pipe collapsed under the driveway and clogged, leaving laundry water to pool in our basement around the floor drain.

A year back I gave up my idea to jackhammer the driveway and developed a plan to get the laundry water into the sewer line where it belongs. The trick is, that sewer line is above your head when you're in the basement, and I'd need a pump to lift the water about seven feet.

I was discussing this with The Mommy when The Boy chimed in.

"I know! I know!" he said. "Maybe we can mark a spot on floor and get The Cat to come over and scratch it up real hard and scratch a hole in the floor, and the water can go down the hole!"

"..."

"Isn't that a great idea?"

"Oh, yeah. That'll work."

I like this. It's a good sign my kid's headed down the same path I'm on — a path lined with tools, gadgets and proposals geared to solving all the world's problems.

I'm a firm believer there's no such thing as a problem that can't be solved, and nothing annoys me more than a problem sitting around gunking up what should otherwise be a fine-tuned universe.

The Boy's heard me pore over problems around the house so much that now he likes to offer advice. But all he comes up with are silly notions like "You should buy a new one." Where's the fun in that?

Fact is, The Boy's solutions haven't been very inventive.

But at least they're not as bad as Monkey's. Monkey, The Boy will tell you, does NOT have good ideas. This may be because he's only a stuffed animal monkey and not a real one. One day we were deciding whether we'd all go to Kroger or split up the errands when The Boy said Monkey had a solution.

"Monkey says we could all walk to Kroger and walk in the middle of the road where the trucks and cars are. He says that's the fastest way. ... It's not a very good idea. Monkey doesn't have very good ideas."

Poor Monkey.

But just when I thought The Boy was about to go the way of the Monkey himself, he surprised me.

Our neighbor, Dr. Frank, has been in a war of wits with local squirrels who raid his bird feeder and scare off his purple finches.

"Dr. Frank!" The Boy shouted. "I know what you can do!"

"What's that?"

"Listen. Here's my idea. You can take the bird feeder down and find a picture of birds and a picture of squirrels and put a picture of birds on one side and a picture of squirrels on the other! So that way they all know where to go! And they won't eat each other's food! Isn't that a great idea?"

Dr. Frank looks at me.

I shrug. "Hey, it's better than what you'll get out of Monkey."

April 9, 2002

Second Baby Sends Daddy into Deep End

As I finished filling the birth tub in our bedroom with hot water, I didn't know what my laboring wife was thinking (probably "All right, it's showtime. Where's my baby?") or what our crowd of a half-dozen cheerleading friends were thinking ("I want to see! I want to see!") or what our midwife was thinking ("There are WAY too many people in this room."). But I do know what I was thinking: "I really don't want to get into that birth tub."

As The Mommy's labor coach, my job was to help her handle contraction pains through massage and some carefully chosen words. We'd done this before, but this was our first time at home and in a rented birth tub, conveniently big enough for two people. The problem is that I don't like getting wet; I'm the only person I know who actually dries the spaces between his toes.

While The Boy ran around checking the floating thermometer, and shouting "I can see The Baby!" (he couldn't), I stayed near The

Mommy's head — where it was dry — and massaged her shoulders and whispered in her ear. I got to stay out of the water for about an hour before she gave me the words I'd been dreading: "I need you to rub my back."

I stepped in, and found that I could do the massage fairly well while standing. Only the bottom inch or so of my shorts was getting soaked, and I could live with that. But she couldn't. On the next contraction I was on my knees, water-logged up to my waist. At least most of my shirt was dry.

Then came pushing.

It turned out the ideal way for The Mommy to push was for me to sit behind her in the tub, holding her up with one leg with her fingers laced between mine. And me up to my neck in water. Now, had I known that home birth would involve me being up to my neck in water, I'd likely have opted to pace the floor in a hospital waiting room. But there was no backing out now, not with a newborn's head crowning, a midwife coaxing, "Easy, easy," The Boy shouting, "Here comes The Baby!" and The Mommy making noises I'd heard only in dark alleys after midnight.

Four hours into labor, with only two pushes, The Baby arrived: 9 pounds, 8 ounces, 22 inches long, and it's a girl. Daddy's girl. A girl for pigtails and ponies, tea parties and proms. And maybe, if we're lucky, she'll be as strong-minded and beautiful as her mother. Amid all the crying and cheering, I could hear The Boy say, "Hi baby sister! I'm your big brother! Hi baby sister! I'm your big brother!"

The Baby was wrapped up, vitals checked, and given to The Mommy, who had been quickly moved to dry clothes and a dry bed. The Boy was filling in all the cheerleaders about his new role as a big brother. I found myself left standing in the birth tub, dripping wet in a murky mix of water and, well, birth fluids.

I believe someone asked me how it felt to be a new daddy again. I'm not sure what I said, but I know exactly what I was thinking: "Can someone hand me a towel?"

April 30, 2002

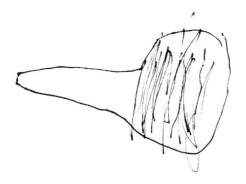

Being a Dad: It's Snot What You'd Expect

We were in our pediatrician's office having a checkup when The Mommy noticed our baby girl had a bit of a glamour problem: A big ol' honkin booger clogging her left nostril.

Our pediatrician wasn't at all dismayed by the booger, or by The Mommy's request that he do something about it.

I was.

I mean, what's he supposed to do? Operate? And then there's that ancient proverb: You can pick your friends, you can pick your nose, but you can't pick your friend's nose.

Well, it turns out, you can pick your friend's nose. The doc told us all you need is "one of those blue ball thingies," which is the technical term for a booger sucker.

He laid The Baby face-up in his lap, resting her head between his knees. He put several drops of saline solution in her nose and she screamed like Jamie Lee Curtis in a mask factory.

She was wailing so loud I couldn't make out what the doc said next, but it was something about mushroom-eating toadstools. In the middle of this chat on fungi and frogs, he squeezed the blue thingie, put the business end in her nose and let go. Her eyes went wide as the thingie went "schnerrrk." She didn't like that either, and notched up the scream to match Janet Leigh at Niagara Falls.

Once he was done, he held her to his shoulder and she quieted down fast, reminding us why we love our pediatrician.

The Baby checked out fine. We left the office with a new blue ball thingie and the confidence that we knew how to use it, though we offered a prayer we'd never have to.

I think God was busy that day, or maybe his ears were still ringing, because within a week The Baby was full-blown sick with a cold. Inevitably, at 4 a.m., her nose was clogged and the blue ball thingie awaited.

I got my saline in arm's reach, got my blue thingie and laid The Baby down, her head between my knees. I dropped in the saline, which dripped all over her face but just shy of her eyes (God heard me that time). With the decibel level at about its peak, I reached for the blue thingie. And she coughed. Her cough somehow came from her nostrils, spraying saline and goo all over my glasses. I deserved that.

But I would not be deterred. I put in the blue thingie and let it rip. "Schnerrrk." Then it hit me that the doctor hadn't been talking about mushroom-eating toadstools at all. He'd said, "Make sure you get a tissue." I hadn't done that, and it was too late now. I squirted the vacuumed snot on my pants leg and went back in for the other nostril. "Schnerrrk." Pants leg again.

I held The Baby to my shoulder. She quieted down and gave me some gentle coos, reminding me why I love being a dad. Some say parenting is all about changing perspective and making sacrifices. Some say it's about changing diapers and doing more laundry — a lot more laundry.

At 4 a.m., blinded by goo and covered in snot, I'd say it's all of the above.

May 14, 2002

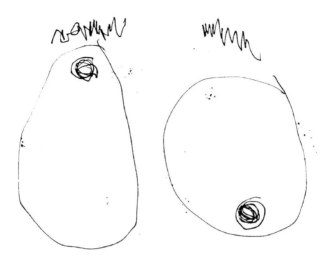

Attack of the Sugar Frosted Syrup Smacks

After mentioning in a recent column that The Boy eats Fiber One cereal, another parent asked me, "You make your kid eat Fiber One?!"

Yes. We lock him in the basement with a glass of murky water and a dry bowl of Fiber One. He's allowed to read the labels on the box only by the dim light filtering under the door.

Truth is, he likes Fiber One. He discovered it one morning after staying the night at Nana's house, which is typical — grandparents always have gross cereal like that around. He tried a bowl and, being a weird kid, he loved it and asked for more.

But I have a confession. Part of the reason he likes Fiber One is that he doesn't exactly know what he's missing.

A long time back The Mommy and I decided there wasn't

much point in feeding our kid Ultra Super Sugar Nitro cereal and Chocolate-Coated Rice-like Syrup O's. Putting all that pre-sweetened, expensive junk on the table is like saying, "Good morning son! Here, have some cake and ice cream. Want some sugar on that?"

Instead, The Boy gets a bagel or toast and plenty of fruit, like an apple, banana, pear or sometimes a bowl of strawberries. Promise you won't report me to social services.

All of this changed last week during a trip down the cereal aisle.

See, The Boy's fallen hard for the Spider-Man hype. He's been jumping around the house saying "Fffpt," shooting imaginary webs and "swinging" from room to room. He hasn't seen the movie and probably won't for a few more years, but all it takes is a newspaper picture to get him going on this sort of thing.

The grocery stores know this, and that's why they stock their most expensive sugary cereal at about 3 feet off the ground — at dead-on eye level for a 4-year-old.

Normally, The Mommy wouldn't let The Boy so much as linger near the Cap'n Crunch, but this time she had The Baby with her, and she's been feeling bad for The Boy, who's suddenly not the center of attention around the house anymore. She saw the box and snatched a chance to spoil him rotten.

"Ooh, look. What's that?"

"Spider-Man!" he said.

Yes, Spider-Man cereal. It consists of cereal bits in the shape of webs that come in three flavors: blue No. 1, red No. 5 and corn syrup.

By Day 3 on this stuff, instead of quietly saying "Fffpt," he was screaming "Spider-Man!" Instead of "swinging" from room to room, he was running top-speed and slamming into the couch, jumping off chairs and rolling on the floor.

The web that broke the spider's back for me was when I saw him jumping around the house, then banging his head into the hard part of our couch. He looked up and laughed like a stoned surfer.

Spider-Man, the cereal, now has a home in the top cabinet above our stove. It might come back down some day. It might not. Meanwhile, we're going back to bagels and bananas, maybe even Fiber One.

I've won the battle for now. But I'm waiting for the war: Any day now "Star Wars" characters should be showing up on bottles of Coke.

May 21, 2002

World Began Not with Bang, but with Bear

I was in a rush to get to work — throwing together a sandwich to go — when The Boy walked in the kitchen with a "Hey Daddy?" Sometimes what follows is a joke. Sometimes it's a request for potato chips. Sometimes it's ... well ... something else.

"What is it Boy?"

"The Aussie Snake was one of the first things ever. Panna Bear made him before there was anything else, like water or animals. He made the Aussie Snake and then he made Sugar Baby. Sugar Baby and Panna Bear were the first things ever."

"Uh, that's great," I said. I gave him a kiss and left for work, then spent the rest of the day trying to figure out just what the heck he was talking about.

The Boy's bound to have a twisted view of the beginning of things. Not long after he was born he was given two books: one a

20-page picture Bible from friends who are Christian missionaries, the other an 8-page children's version of Darwin's "Origin of Species" from friends who are amused atheists. We like to display the books side-by-side.

And now, somehow, these readings have combined with Sunday school and, I suspect, Disney's "Hercules" to generate a creation story centered on two of his favorite stuffed animals — Sugar Baby and Panna Bear.

But what the heck is an Aussie Snake?

Over dinner I asked for a better explanation.

"Aussie Snake comes from Aussie Planet. Panna Bear made that first, after the monsters." Aussie Planet? I wondered if he meant Australia Planet, which would match his other claim that there's gold buried on Planet Africa, an idea he must have gotten from all that 1970s funk music he's been listening to.

The Mommy solved the mystery. Turns out he isn't saying "Aussie" but "RC." It's from a commercial for a remote-controlled plastic snake you use to terrify your sister.

OK, RC Snake comes from RC Planet. But how did Panna Bear get to be god of the universe?

Well, actually, creation is still in revision.

"Skull and Ol' Hookhand got the stars made. They were the first gods and the goodest gods on earth. They could fly too."

Skull and Ol' Hookhand, for those who haven't yet seen the light, are plastic toy pirates.

"They decided to make a frog planet, then they blasted up the alien frogs. These were the first things before dinosaurs. Sugar Baby and Panna Bear were after the dinosaurs. Then they died and were made into stuffed animals."

That's it then. My son is going to hell. All these Sundays of keeping him calm in church, all the Bible story readings, even his baptism, all for nothing. Not only does he believe the world was created by pirates, he's a polytheistic idolater. And worse: evolution.

But this can't be right. How could a pair of 2-inch tall pirates with Fisher-Price stamped on their feet create the universe? And if they're so powerful, why does one have an eyepatch and the other a missing hand?

But we ask too many questions. Religion is an act of faith.

"Yeah. Ol' Hookhand is the most powerful," The Boy summarized, with the assurance of a true believer. "He's powerfuller than anybody. ... Except Jesus."

Well that's good, but we're still sending him to vacation Bible school.

July 2, 2002

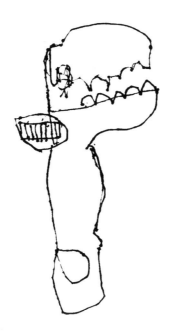

Dad's No Good with a Bad Back

B end with your knees.
 I've heard that nag since sixth grade gym class and I've ignored it almost as long. In my first high school job I hefted boxes of liquor and raised trays of food over my head, putting all the weight on my back. It's the sensible thing to do — I've never been Mr. Atlas, but my back is long and broad, so I work with what I've got.

Or had.

Last month I decided to fix a leaky shower faucet. It's a simple job, if your pipes aren't fused by decades of corrosion, and of course mine were. This called for my 14-inch pipe wrench (the kind Col. Mustard used to whack Professor Plum). On the final stubborn pipe, I put my whole back into it, and managed a quarter turn before I realized I was pulling the wrong way, tightening the pipe. After muttering some words daddies say only during home maintenance projects, I stood up to change positions.

My back stayed where it was.

A big bucket of "daddy words" spewed out, but this time I didn't mutter. This kind of pain was payback for all those years of dead-lifting grocery bags, moving boxes and 4-year-olds.

For the first few days, I did a lot of whining at work and at home. Of course the usual reply wasn't the compassion I clearly deserved, but instead, "Did you take any aspirin?" Now, why would I take aspirin? My back only hurts when I use it, and the cure for that is to complain until someone says, "Oh you poor thing," and then I feel better.

But not using my back isn't so easy. I never knew how much daddies need their backs.

The worst of it is picking up The Baby. I've tried every angle and position to lift her from her crib without swallowing bursts of pain, but there's no way around it. When it's my turn for the middle-of-the-night feeding, The Mommy hears two cries: one from The Baby and one from me, often with a few daddy words tossed in.

Then there's The Boy. It used to be when he fell asleep in the car I'd get him out and carry him in the house then up the stairs, lying him gently in his bed. Heck, now I can't bend over to unbuckle his car seat. And you can forget about horsey rides.

During a recent light saber battle, I fell to the floor, "wounded," and my back decided we should stay there.

"Come on, Daddy, get up," The Boy said.

"Actually, I'm defeated. I'm just going to lie here dead for a while. Or maybe I could fight you from here."

"No, you should get up and play again."

"Well, you see, my back hurts," I said, hoping for some sympathy from the only person who seemed to care.

"Hmm," he said. "Probably you should get a Band-Aid or take some medis-nin and you would feel more better."

Y'know, one of these days my back will really be hurt and people will have to care. My son will have to help me up off the floor. The Mommy will kiss me and say, "Oh, you poor thing." Maybe I'll even get a sympathy card.

OK, OK. I'll go take an aspirin.

July 9, 2002

Cherry Tree Lesson Isn't Working Out

At about 11 p.m. while enjoying a movie with The Mommy, I heard something. I paused the VCR and listened. It was the sound of water running, so either The Baby was doing dishes or The Boy was getting a nightcap. We went back to the movie. A minute or so later I realized the water was still running. Maybe The Baby really was doing dishes. I stopped the movie and went upstairs, where I discovered The Boy, standing on his stool, diligently washing his hands.

"What are you doing?"

"Why are you washing your ..." Then I saw his hands, covered in blue ink.

"Well," he explained. "The problem is, I think the lid came off the marker."

He turned to look at me with ink-stained lips.

"And then I couldn't find the lid anywhere."

"Boy, open your mouth." Yep, there was ink on his tongue. He may not have been sniffin' markers, but he was definitely tasting them.

As The Boy continued washing his hands — which wasn't doing any good, by the way — I called The Mommy upstairs; I knew she'd want to hear this one.

"Where else did you color?" she asked, not sure she wanted an answer.

"Well, I wanted to color my toes."

Yes, his toes were blue.

"OK. Where else did you color?"

"Places where you couldn't see."

"Can you show me?" The Mommy asked.

"Yeah!" he said proudly. There was the edge of his bookshelf, the underside of his bed and the underbodies of some Matchbox cars. So The Boy's figured out how to be devious, but he still wasn't clear on the concept of lying about it, not yet anyway.

We explained that markers are for using on paper, not on furniture, not on cars and not as mouthwash. The markers were confiscated — placed off limits in the art closet. But we commended him for confessing his sins, tucked him in and muffled our laughter as we went back to our movie.

A couple of days later, The Mommy found an art project on a table in the den. It was a piece of cut paper folded over and sealed with red wax. Impressive, but how exactly was the paper cut? The Mommy soon discovered her big pointy scrapbooking scissors were put back in the wrong place — he'd used them without permission or supervision, and you could put an eye out with those things. When she asked him about it, he told us his first, bona-fide, flat-out lie: "Daddy said I could play with them."

OK, what now? Beat him? Take his car keys? We'd never discussed how to handle lying, because we didn't figure he'd try it so soon. In the absence of any better ideas, we sent him to his room so we could think up a good punishment.

"Wuaaah!" Screaming and gnashing of teeth shook every timber of the house as he trudged up the stairs. Well, that settled that.

But then there was something extra: Upon breaking the seal on his art project we found a design he'd colored using, that's right, a contraband blue marker, carefully put back in the art closet afterwards, but not quite in the right place.

Did George Washington's parents ever have days like this?

July 16, 2002

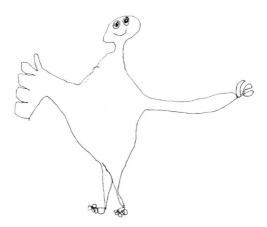

There's More to Baby Than a 'Goodgie' Face

"Aw, isn't she cute?"
"Oh, she's just goodgie-goo oh yes!"

These and other descriptions have been applied to my daughter since about five seconds after she left the womb. I'm flattered (except for that weird "goodgie-goo" bit), because she looks just like me and her mother, which is further proof that I have excellent taste in wives.

But these descriptions aren't specific. Sure she's "beeuw-teeful" (as my New Jersey grand-mother puts it), but in what way?

Having spent a fair amount of time observing The Baby, I have some more accurate descriptions:

• Bobbleheaded. Remember those cheap plastic toys from the 1960s with oversized heads on springs that would wobble around for no apparent reason? That's pretty much her. Kind of like Ray Charles, but without rhythm. The best of it, though, is when she's shimmying around and suddenly gains control. When she stiffens up, she gives you a stunned look as if to say, "Where the heck did you come from?"

• Gum-faced. Finally, she's begun to smile. Well, if you count an open-mouthed, toothless grin as a smile. Her eyes brighten up, her little cheeks pull back and she shows you her two rows of glistening pink gums. This is cute only in babies, by the way, so please Mrs. Florenstein, don't get any ideas.

• Bubble-bearded. One of the greatest joys in her small life is to purse her lips together and blow tiny spit bubbles, which tend to collect on her chin until she comes to resemble a small bearded man. Sometimes she adds sound effects, little "spbfft"'s, which, if she had that Ray Charles rhythm going, might make for a good rap act: MC Small Bearded Man.

• Jabber-talkin. Speaking of rap, The Baby has inherited her mother's passion for talking, and she likes to share this with me at 6 a.m. during diaper changes. Let's see, there's "Grhl" for "girl," "Guhdz" for "gourds," "Hoom" for "whom," "Gtda" for "Daddy," "La" for "Linguistics," "Yai" for "Aye-aye captain" and "Bzz-ah" for "Wonderful Daddy." I mean, look at that. You can't tell me babies don't know how to communicate. (The Mommy, by the way, thinks these words mean something totally different, but she's obviously mistranslating.)

• Googley-eyed. The Boy loves to point this out, and greets his sister every morning by commenting, "She's so googley-eyed today." But he's right, particularly when the lights are dim. I noticed it the first week after she was born as I was walking her around the house trying to get her to sleep. When I was in a room with bright lights, she'd barely squint. As I moved into a darker room, her eyes got wider and wider until she was bug-eyed as Sugar-Baby (The Boy's nocturnal mammal-like toy). I tried this experiment again recently, dimming and brightening the lights as The Baby ate. Amid The Mommy's protests for me to stop torturing my children, I noticed how when the lights got dim, she'd open her eyes so wide you could actually see the whites all the way around. Yep. Googley-eyed.

So that's the perfect description of my daughter: Bobbleheaded, gum-faced, bubble-bearded, jabber-talkin, googley-eyed and beeuw-teeful.

July 30, 2002

Bad News: Boy's Electric to Blueberries

In about six weeks, we're going to visit my mom in Florida. So, of course, The Boy has just discovered he's electric to blueberries.

Confused? So are we.

All this started a couple of years back when The Boy was learning to walk. He managed to hit his head on coffee tables, chairs, whatever would work to give him shiners across his brow. All this just before we went to visit my mom, who used to work in Child Protective Services and is trained to look for signs of abuse. She would love an excuse to keep one of her grandchildren, so we were nervous we'd be coming back one kid short.

We got home as a trio, but several months later, just in time for our next visit to Mimi's, The Boy took a spill on his scooter. This time it was his chin — a nasty scrape that ended up leaving a scar. Another injury, just in time for Mimi's inspection.

Leading up to the next visit — my sister's wedding — we treated that child like a glass trophy. I installed bumpers on all the furniture corners in the house and the scooter was temporarily off limits. As we pulled into the wedding site parking lot and waved to my mom, I thought, "Finally, she'll see that he's not constantly covered in cuts and bruises."

As she began walking toward me, I set The Boy down in the parking lot. He took one step, then slammed his forehead into the asphalt. Yes, there was blood.

It's been a couple of years since The Boy prefaced each Mimi visit by banging into the walls for a week, but still, I get nervous. And now, he's electric to blueberries.

Actually, it may not be the blueberries.

One afternoon, over a bowl of blueberries, The Boy started scratching. I figured it was mosquito bites. The Mommy took a closer look, and found raised patchy welts all over his arm. Uh-oh. Poison ivy. That afternoon, while eating more blueberries for lunch, The Boy was still itching, but this time it was his leg. Sure enough, there were raised patches on his leg, but the patches on his arm were gone.

This wasn't poison ivy, this was hives. The Mommy suggested a possible allergy, and ever since, if you ask The Boy about his hives, he's likely to say, "Yeah, I'm electric to blueberries."

OK, there's no way we can let Mimi see The Boy with welts on his face or she'll have the police at her house before we unpack our bags. (That's actually pretty easy since my stepdad's a cop.) So we had to figure out the allergy and quick. We put away the blueberries, but that didn't work. Then we tried cutting out milk, and it seemed to help.

Then we noticed the hives were worse when he first woke up, so we set up a fan in his room upstairs. Bingo. Turns out he was getting overheated at night, and the heat was causing him to either break out in hives or be more susceptible to allergies.

Whew. Now all we have to do is keep him out of the heat ... during our trip to Florida. If we come back less one child, don't worry — you can reach him at Mimi's.

August 6, 2002

Daddy Takes Leap Into Dark Socks

I walked in the kitchen to take out the garbage and was greeted with guffaws from The Mommy.

"How old are you?" she asked

"Why?"

"Dark socks with shorts?"

I looked down. Yep. Dark socks with shorts. I still had on my work socks from yesterday and was about to take a shower, so there wasn't much point in changing socks just for a 30-second trip to the back yard ... except to keep my wife from thinking I'm ready to retire to Tampa and vote AARP.

This is yet another sign that I'm turning wholly into a daddy. When I look at pictures of myself from college — wearing some bohemian shirt, arguing about art and philosophy with a cigarette hanging out of my mouth — I wonder if that guy knew that one day he'd walk outside with a bag of trash, wearing dark socks with shorts.

For those of you who haven't gotten to the daddy stage yet, here are some things you have to look forward to, or maybe beware of:

- Soggy shoulder. It starts with a bit of spit-up. As they get older, babies get more generous, shifting to drool. Then unwiped chins bring baby food to the palette. All of this gets emblazoned on your left shoulder, I think as some sort of baby territory-marking to warn other infants that you're taken.
- Potty mouth. Topics that once made you queasy and want to leave the room suddenly are as easy to discuss as the weather, but much more interesting. From what I can tell, the queasiness comes back once the kids grow up (and if you don't believe that, you should hear some of the comments I got on the stuffy nose column).
- Letting yourself go. I used to worry a lot more about how I look — about the image I project. As has become clear with the dark socks, I don't have nearly as much time for that sort of thing anymore. I'm not the only one. I have a picture at home of a Navy officer friend of mine wearing a princess hat with his daughters. Another guy I know — a big guy you'd picture being at home on a football field — has confessed to me his regular attendance at tea parties. The rock 'n' roll lifestyle it ain't.
- Borrowing products. One of my co-workers the other day was accused of smelling like a baby. She demanded to know exactly what part of a baby she smelled like. The single male reporter said, "I don't know. Just a baby." Then it hit her: She needed moisturizer when getting ready for work that morning and grabbed the baby lotion. If it works it works — doesn't much matter whose cabinet it came from. The same applies to Sparkle Fun Kid's Crest toothpaste (blue flavor), Winnie the Pooh cran-apple-orange-berry juice boxes and old cloth diapers (they make great oil rags). But I draw the line at baby food. If God wanted hot dogs to be pureed, he'd have made them that way.

Men, this is what you have to look forward to. Stay strong and be prepared for the big change. Of course, some of you won't have as much trouble, particularly if you've always wanted to wear princess hats at tea parties and have a taste for Gerber teething biscuits.

August 20, 2002

Spontaneous Romance? Ha Ha Ha!

One of the hardest things to get used to when you become a daddy is the disappearance of, well, "romance." There was a time when, with nothing more than a certain look, The Mommy and I would run off together and get the birds a singin' and the bees a buzzin'. But with kids in the picture, that certain look also requires a Month-at-a-Glance Day Planner and synchronized watches.

Last week The Mommy and I struggled to find time to ourselves. Finally, I had a day off, and everything was set. We'd have dinner, take the kids for a walk to wear them out, put them to bed, watch a romantic movie while they fell asleep, then create some romance of our own.

Well, dinner and getting out the door take a lot longer with kids, so by the time we got to the riverfront park, it was about 8 p.m. We're night people anyway, so this wasn't a problem for us. But I think it was for the couples strolling by, giggling, kissing and giving each another those certain looks. I'm sure they loved hearing The Boy run by shouting, "That barge sure is stinky!"

Oh, yes, there was the barge. Our quiet night was interrupted by its constant drone, so we had to yell the whole time. Then The Baby got bored, and her fussing forced us back to the car. By the time we got home, The Mommy and I were more worn out than the kids.

But we would not be deterred.

I fixed coffee while The Mommy put The Baby to bed and started The Boy's bedtime stories. He wanted two. Then there were prayers and my obligatory carrying him to bed.

Breathless now, but only from the haul upstairs, I cuddled up with The Mommy to watch "Xiu Xiu: The Sent Down Girl," what appeared to be the moving tale of a Chinese girl who falls in love with a horse trainer in a pastoral paradise.

Not exactly.

About the time we found out that the horse trainer is impotent, The Baby woke up. So she watched the movie with us for about an hour, and seemed as surprised as we were when the girl became a prostitute. Oh yeah sure, that's romantic.

Just as our movie was starting to unravel — and just as my coffee was wearing off — The Baby fell asleep. We put her to bed. Now, here's the point where I should have turned off the movie, gazed lovingly into my wife's eyes and commenced to romancin'. What did we do? Went back to watching the movie. We got another half-hour in before I noticed a 4-year-old blond head pop around the corner.

"Daddy?" The Boy said, walking in with Monkey under one arm. "I'm hungry."

Inside I screamed. "Boy, what are you doing out of bed?"

"Well, I wasn't hungry for dinner before, but now I was thinking maybe I could have some cheese."

"I was thinking maybe you should go back to sleep."

I walked him up the stairs and got back to the movie just in time for the horse trainer to kill the girl, then himself.

It's not "9 1/2 Weeks," but it would have to do.

August 27, 2002

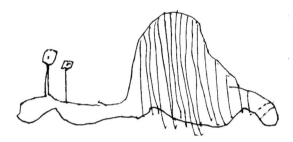

Conch Tossing a Total Blast for The Boy

It was a working vacation for The Boy. We spent a week at the beach with my family, diving for scallops, cleaning scallops and eating scallops. This was heaven for me and The Mommy, and beyond heaven for my mom, who got to spend most of her waking hours holding The Baby.

But for The Boy? Well, we had a bit of a time finding stuff for him to do. He doesn't like scallops or putting his head underwater, much less spooning the nasty stuff out a scallop shell.

So we put him to work.

It was his job to carry one of the scallop nets to and from the dock, and to help Papa fix the ladder on the back of the boat. I'm not sure what was involved in doing this, but Papa tells me it kept The Boy happy for the whole hour we were diving around scallop beds.

He was also in charge of throwing "stupidconchs" caught in our crab trap back into the gulf. (I think he heard it "stupid conchs" often enough from Papa that he decided it must be one word.)

But past that, I was worried he wasn't having much of a vacation.

One night, when he'd taken a late nap then wasn't sleepy at bedtime, he came out on the porch where we adults were gathered for our nightly talk. We have this tradition of gathering in a circle out-of-doors, drinking wine and beer and yakking about our memories and dreams, then arguing about constellations.

In the middle of such a session, The Boy peeped his head out the back door and said, "Probably if someone will fix me a cup of milk I'll come hang out with you guys."

The next day I decided I had to find something he'd really enjoy. We went to the beach, such as it was. The area we were in has no sandy beaches. Instead, it's half-sand, half-mud and half-grass, which adds up to 150 percent muck. At low tide the waveless water is about eight inches deep for at least the length of a football field from the shore.

At first, The Boy's reaction was much the same as mine: "Gross!" But I didn't voice my opinion, and I coaxed him (well, picked him up and hauled him) out into the water. After a bit of whining, he got used to it and took to pretending he was a three-clawed dinosaur stomping around making swirling sand clouds in the water at his feet.

The sun was setting, and before long I found myself experiencing a perfect moment. The Boy was running in circles, whooping and yelling about monsters and heroes. He ran across a still plane of water, flat and shallow, extending out to the luscious, quiet purple sunset behind him.

He wasn't bored. He was having the time of his life, only I was too worried about whether he was having fun to see that carrying nets, fixing ladders and tossing conchs is, for him, a total blast.

He ran up and chased me out of my thoughts, screaming he'd gnash me up with his T-rex teeth and claws. I let him chase me until he tripped in the water, soaking his shorts. Instead of the angry cries I expected, he laughed.

By instinct, he knew the whole point to enjoying a vacation, a point I'd missed in trying to make it perfect: Relax.

September 10, 2002

The Quiet Life Isn't Always by Choice

"You're awfully quiet tonight," The Mommy said.

We'd stopped at a restaurant on the way back from vacation and the kids were restless from about six hours in the car.

"Well," I said, "I was just thinking about that, actually."

"About what, Daddy?" The Boy said.

"About being quiet."

"How is everything?" the waiter asked.

"Great!" The Boy said.

"Ahhhragala," The Baby said.

I nodded. "I was thinking about ..."

"Hey Daddy can I have some more toast instead of my macaroni?"

"No, eat your macaroni. ... I was thinking about being quiet and how I was raised."

"What do you mean?" The Mommy asked.

"But Dad, what if my macaroni is being mean to me."

"All the more reason to eat it."

"So anyway," The Mommy said.

"So anyway, I think I was raised to be quiet ..."

"AaaAAAAAGGGAaa!" The Baby said.

"AaAAAAHHHGG-GGHHHAAaaa!"

"BABY! BE QUIET!" The Boy shouted, drawing looks from the entire restaurant.

"Boy," I said, doing the Mean Daddy look but trying not to shout, "We. Will. Handle. The. Baby. Eat. Your. Mac. A. Roni."

The Mommy found a toy for The Baby to gnaw on. "So, you think you were raised to be quiet?"

"Oh, that. Yeah. Because my sisters and mom were so talkative, I think I found myself ..."

"Hey there, little lady!" A random waiter stopped by. "You get that toy! Yeah, you get it! Hey folks, she's a doll!" I think he actually pointed his finger and clicked at us as he walked off.

"Thanks. ... So I found myself being talked over all the time and struggling to get ..."

"Eww, Mommy, she spit up!"

"No, honey, that's just drool."

"But it's all over Daddy's arm!"

"Daddy doesn't care," I said. "Eat your macaroni."

"Here, let me get a napkin," The Mommy said, rummaging in the diaper bag.

"No, I'm fine, really."

"I'm done eating anyway," she said. "You want me to hold her while you finish?"

"Uh, sure, OK." I passed The Baby across the table.

"Come here little girl!" The Mommy cooed. "How you doin? Are you happy to see Mommy? Yes you are."

"AaaaAAAAHHHaaaagala."

"... so she had one foot on Papa's boat and one foot off Papa's boat." The Boy was talking to the couple in the table behind us. "And she was going to fall in the water or her legs were going to break off and get eaten by fishes."

"I'm sorry," I said to the couple.

"No, that's fine. We're enjoying this, really."

"So," The Mommy said, "you think you were raised to be quiet?"

"How would you folks like some dessert?"

"... and the fish had light sabers and googley eyes!"

"AaaaHAAAAGAGAgalagala."

"Check, please."

September 17, 2002

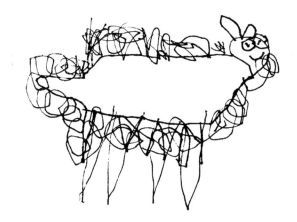

Monsters No Match for Lambie-Pie

After working late at the office I got home long after all the bedtime stories, prayers and tuckings-in. Everyone, including The Mommy, was asleep — or so I thought.

I walked in the dimly lit playroom and began putting away my things, then looked up to see The Boy sitting on the couch staring at me.

"Gaah!"

"Hi Daddy."

I deserved that. When I was a kid if I woke up in the middle of the night with a bad dream I'd go to my parents' room and stand silently next to the bed until my mom woke up, scared out of her pajamas, to herd me back to my room.

"What are you doing down here?" I asked The Boy.

"Well you see," he said, "it's boring upstairs so I thought maybe I'd come sleep in the prayloom." (Yes, the "prayloom." We'll cry the day he says it right.)

He was curled up on the couch wrapped in a blanket.

"Well, you need to go back to bed."

"Daddy, I think there's some ghosts and monsters making shadows in my room."

"There are? Hmm. What are we going to do?"

"We should put on armor and shields and go investigate," he said, shaking his fist for emphasis.

So that's what we did.

He has a helmet and a red felt tunic that apparently protect him from laser blasts, dragon breath — that sort of thing. All I got was a wooden shield, but he assured me that would be enough. I grabbed a plastic broom just in case.

We crept up the stairs, saying nothing above a whisper for fear of alerting the monsters around the corner. Suddenly we heard the clatter of a chain dragging across the floor! Wait. ... Actually that was just The Mommy snoring.

In his room The Boy pointed out the shadows that were bugging him. One of them was from a toy bunny in front of his nightlight.

I helped him out of his armor and tucked him in.

Then he wanted me to make up story. I was about to tell him enough's enough — it was way past any memory of bedtime and he needed to hush up and go to sleep. But a story hit me:

"Once upon a time there was a little boy who was worried about monsters and couldn't fall asleep. So he gathered all his stuffed animals around him on the bed. Some of those animals had been keeping him safe since he was a little baby, and they loved him with all their might. So they watched over him that night and made sure he could sleep safe and comfy. The End."

"That's a good story, Dad."

Ah, a perfect daddy moment. On my way out of the room, as

I was straining my arm to pat myself on the back, The Boy said, "Hey Daddy?"

"Yeah?"

"Can you turn on the big ceiling light for me? 'Cause I'm still kinda worried."

OK, so maybe the story didn't work perfectly. But when I came up later to turn off the light, he had one arm around Lambie-Pie and another around the purple platypus. Those monsters don't stand a chance.

September 24, 2002

Rub a Dub-Dub Don't Let Dad Near the Tub

Every now and then, to keep myself out of trouble, I ask The Mommy if she wants some help — making lunch, changing a diaper, brushing "the bugs" out of The Boy's teeth. The usual response is "No, I've got it. Thanks."

But this weekend I goofed. I had a beer with dinner and was in an unusually relaxed and jovial mood, which played nicely off the exhausted and frazzled mood The Mommy was in. Without much thought, I offered, half-joking of course, that I'd give the kids a bath.

"Actually," she said, before I could take it back, "that would be great."

What I meant to say, I said only to myself, is that if you're ever laid up with West Nile virus and the kids are so filthy we have to have their hair de-matted — I'll give the kids a bath. But it was too late, The Mommy was off to the sofa for a well-deserved hour with a novel. Or so she thought.

"All right, kids," I said. "Go take a bath."

The Boy objected. "But I don't know how to turn the things so the water is not too hot and not too cold."

The Baby sucked for a moment on a plastic blue moon toy, giving the matter some thought, then looked up at me as if to say, "Gah?"

Twenty minutes later, with a lot of help from The Mommy, I was all set. The Baby was in her bath seat in the tub, sucking on a wet rag. The Boy was waist-deep in a pirate rescue adventure.

I got to scrubbing, and found that getting shampoo and soap on a baby is easy enough. Getting the soap off? Not so easy.

"Hey Mommy," I called downstairs.

"Yes?"

"How do I get the soap off of her?"

There was a pause, and I think I heard her counting to 10. "With water," she said.

So I gave it a shot, and managed to trickle soapy water all over her eyes and mouth. She sputtered a bit and looked up as if to ask, "Gah?"

I rinsed off the rest of the soap that I could see, but now for the slippery baby-fat folds. Underarms, OK, easy enough. Under the neck. ... Hmm.

"Hey Mommy."

"Yes?"

"How do I rinse the soap from under of her neck?"

"With difficulty," she said.

That wasn't encouraging. "Hey Baby! Hey! Look up here!" I said, trying to trick her into raising her head. "Hey! Woo-hoo!" I clapped my hands and whistled and clicked, glad the bathroom window wasn't facing the street. Nothing.

"Probably you should turn her upside down," The Boy said.

The Baby looked up to smile at her brother, just enough for me to slip the wet rag under her neck.

OK, clean baby, clean boy. "Everybody out of the tub!"

The Baby looked at me and sucked her rag, as if to say, "You forgot my towels. I ain't goin' anywhere."

Oh. "Hey Mommy."

More counting. "Yes?"

"I forgot The Baby's towels."

And that was the end of The Mommy's novel.

Once it was all over, I was exhausted. But the kids were clean, and I learned a lot. Lesson No. 1: Getting in trouble is easier than bathing the kids.

October 1, 2002

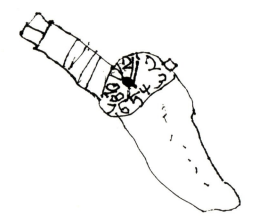

Half the Trip is Getting Out the Front Door

The Halloween costume this year came down to a choice between cool-but-complicated and boring-but-quick. At first The Boy was going to be Luke Skywalker. Then he saw something about dressing up as a ghost and changed his mind. As the deadline approached, we tried to change his mind back — we'd been wanting to do a Star Wars theme for years. It would take a lot more time, but it'd be worth it.

The Boy came over to our side, so long as there was a light saber in it for him.

"OK, then," I said, noticing it was already 12:30 and we'd have to go buy materials if we wanted to start making the costumes that day. "Let's get going."

"I'll change The Baby while you get dressed and put The Boy's shoes on," The Mommy offered.

"OK. Boy, go find your shoes."

I untangled the laces and shoed The Boy.

"Hey Daddy, I'm kinda hungry. Can I have a peanut butter and honey sandwich?"

"Uh, sure. Hey, Mommy! We need to eat lunch real quick."

"I'll need to feed her, then."

I fixed a sandwich for The Boy, and while The Baby had a bottle, I packed the diaper bag. Somewhere in there I started getting dressed. Then The Boy came in, covered in peanut butter and honey.

"Daddy, I think I need a napkin."

I washed him up, combed his hair and began brushing his teeth. Five seconds into it he started squirming.

"You have to go potty, don't you?"

"Rrm-hrm," he said, mouth full of toothpaste. This happens every time — you'd think one of us would remember.

He peed. I brushed. He rinsed and I finished getting dressed. The Mommy came in and started flipping through shirts in her closet. She was changing clothes. Then it hit me: I was hungry. I went to the kitchen and scarfed down the remnants of The Boy's sandwich.

"OK," I shouted to the house, "let's get in the car."

I walked in the playroom and found The Boy playing nicely ... without shoes. "Why did you take your shoes off?"

"Is it time to go?" he asked.

"It's been time to go for an hour and a half! OK, sit down; I'll put them back on."

The Mommy came in and said she'd be right there after she changed The Baby's diaper.

"Isn't this where we started?" I asked. I finished re-shoeing The Boy and told him to stand still while I tracked down my keys. I found The Mommy going through The Baby's drawer, looking for a new shirt.

"What are you doing?" I asked.

"She was crawling on the floor and now her shirt's all dirty."

Suddenly I realized where I was: I was in a play. It was Side B of "Waiting For Godot."

"OK, that's it. Her shirt's fine. You're ready. I'm ready. The Boy's ready. The Baby's ready. Let's go."

We made it to the car without further incident, and as we pulled away The Mommy and I came to a decision: This year, we were buying four sheets and a pair of scissors. Ghosts would do just fine.

October 22, 2002

Storm Calmed By Questions, Oreos

We never used to worry much about weather — we often ignored tropical storm hysteria in Florida — until we moved to Clarksville just after the 1999 tornado and got a good look at what was left of downtown, particularly the newsroom I'd be working at and the church we'd be worshiping in. Now we hustle to the basement at the first word of warning.

So earlier this week when the tornado sirens started wailing, we didn't wait to look for funnel clouds.

The Mommy raced upstairs to wake The Boy, whose sleepy-eyed response was, "OK. ... Let me get Sugar Baby." Stuffed animal in tow and sock-footed, he crept down to our unfinished basement and found a spot on an old couch I've yet to haul away.

One child down, one to go. I got The Baby in her carrier and to the basement without waking her, and I'd just put her carrier on the floor when The Boy yelled his first question of the night: "Daddy is she asleep?"

Well, not anymore.

The Baby didn't fall back asleep, but at least she calmed down. I, however, was a wreck. Between The Boy's steady stream of questions ("Why is our back deck red?" "Why does the volcano make the trees go wobbly?") and the steady stream of water creating a puddle around our flooded floor drain, I was a bit tense.

The Mommy suggested I go grab a beer and some food. I came back down with a bag of Oreos and found a place on the springless couch with The Boy. We didn't share the beer, but we did share the cookies and a lot more questions. ("Why can a volcano hurt us?" "Why does God make floods?")

Once the storm passed we put the kids back to bed and The Mommy fielded the final two questions. ("Will the volcano still be happening when I wake up?" "Will our church still be here in the morning?")

The next day I was telling my older sister what a terrible night we had, and she reminded me of a similar night almost 30 years ago. I was woken by police sirens on our street and an officer on a bullhorn commanding everyone to seek shelter.

We were the only ones in our subdivision with a half-underground garage, so all the neighbors came over to take refuge with us. My mom brought down a pot of coffee, and a dozen or more grownups — some concerned, some distracted — stood around chatting while us kids played in stacks of old cardboard boxes up until what must've been midnight.

This week's tornado also was terrifying, in fact, deadly. But I wonder if The Boy will keep a memory of watching the trees blow sideways as he sat on a broken couch with Sugar Baby and his dad, eating Oreos and asking questions.

If he does, I hope he also keeps the same sense I had of feeling safe. Not because you have any reason to feel that way — not with winds ripping around your home and lightning crackling the air — but simply because you trust someone enough to believe them when they say everything's going to be all right.

November 12, 2002

Fox Family Has Exciting Thanksgiving

In honor of the holiday, here's 4-year-old's Thanksgiving story sure to warm your heart, or at least remind you not to overcook the turkey.

"Once upon time there were three ... um ..."

"Three what?" I asked.

"Um, pause this story a second and let me think," The Boy said. "OK hit play again. There were three foxes: A daddy fox, a mommy fox, a little boy fox and a baby fox."

"I think that's four," I said.

"Yes, four foxes. And they were eating some Thanksgiving dinner, but it was too hot, so the daddy fox decided maybe it would be good to go outside. Now, the daddy fox, he wasn't very smart."

"Oh, he wasn't?"

"No, he wasn't. But the little boy fox, he was smarter than the daddy. And the daddy fox said, 'OK, guys let's go outside!' But the little boy fox said, 'Daddy I think it's too cold. We need jackets and socks.' But the daddy fox said, 'No, we'll be just fine!' But the little boy fox said, 'Daddy I think it's too windy.' But the daddy fox said, 'No, we'll be just fine!'"

"So, the little boy fox was real smart?"

"No, he wasn't really," The Boy said. "But he was smarter than his daddy."

"Oh, great."

"So the daddy fox went to the door, and he opened the door and said, 'See it's just fine,' and he stepped outside, and a big wind blasted him away! And he said, 'Aaagh!' So the little boy fox ran to the door and said, 'I'll save you Daddy!' and he grabbed his daddy's tail. But then the little boy fox started to fly away, so the mommy fox ran and grabbed the little boy fox's tail. And she started to fly away, and soon all that was left was the little baby fox!"

"Oh, no!"

"Yes, so the little baby fox went to the door, and she slammed it shut."

"What?!"

"Yeah. She's actually a very bad baby," The Boy said.

"That's terrible!"

"But then she heard them all yelling, so she got some jackets and some mittens and some hot Coca-Cola and took it outside to them and got them all warm."

"Well, good," I said. "Is that the end?"

"No ... because suddenly ... there was a bear behind them, and it said, 'Graargh!' And they were so scared because the bear had big branches for arms with skulls hanging from them."

"Good grief! Is that a tree-bear monster or something?"

"... No, Daddy. It's just a bear."

"Oh, OK. Please continue."

"But then, suddenly, the foxes looked, and behind the bear

there was something else. Something big, with red, glowing eyes. And it had a light saber."

The tale drifted off into a series of confused battle scenes, and from what I could make out, the Fox family went home to finish dinner. After about 10 minutes of this, The Boy said, "The End."

"Did you like my story, Daddy?"

"Yes," I said. "I thought it was great, particularly the part about the little boy fox rescuing his daddy."

"And if you ever need me to rescue you next time, tell me and I'll rescue you, OK?"

"OK," I said. "Thanks."

November 26, 2002

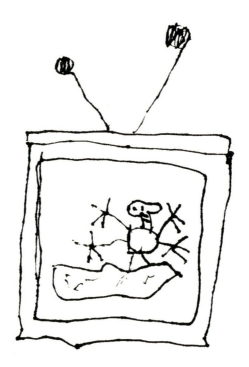

Pay Attention to that Cricket, Boy

"Lilo & Stitch" looks harmless enough. It's your typical Disney story: A dangerous space alien is adopted (under the guise of being a dog) by a lonely Hawaiian orphan. I think Annette Funicello did a flick like this once.

But about 30 minutes into it, the little orphan, Lilo—a kindergartner — tells a guy her sister "likes your butt." A running gag in the movie is Stitch calling everyone "stupidhead." This may not seem like a big deal, but I know my kid, and now my kid is going to think it's funny to call his grandmother "stupidhead," and talk about people's butts at the library.

You think he won't? The Boy learned from "Aladdin" that it's funny to be annoyingly rude ("What's your problem?"). He learned from "Star Wars: Phantom Menace" that it's OK for little boys to talk back to adults. ("OK, OK, I'm going!") He learned from "Monsters, Inc." that loud belching is a riot (I might have helped him along, but that's beside the point).

More than once he's thrown a "light saber" at me and said, "Meet your destiny."

No matter how good a movie's message, The Boy will pick up all the behavior he sees, whether it's from Stuart Little or Snowbell, Darth Vader or Luke, Pooh or Rabbit, the Grinch or Cindy-Lou Who.

In fact, the bad guys have the best lines in all those movies. Who wants to mumble with Pooh, "A little more honey, please," when you could instead shout with Rabbit, "Get that bear out of my house!"

Luckily, though, we also have Jiminy Cricket.

After The Boy saw "Pinocchio," there were a couple of points he wasn't clear on, like why did Geppetto not already have a little boy of his own? Why can the wolf talk, but not the cats or donkeys? Why can't I whistle? Those were easy next to the big question:

"Mommy, what's a conscience?"

The Mommy thought for a moment and came up with this: "It's that little voice inside your head that warns you when you're about to do something bad."

The Boy thought for a moment. "... I don't hear anything."

It took some explaining before The Mommy could clear up the difference between having a conscience and having hallucinations, but it seems to have sunk in. A few days later at dinner the rest of us were almost done, but The Boy was doing more talking than eating. I told him fill his mouth with more food and fewer words.

"Oh, yeah? Well I ..."

He stopped himself. I pushed it a little: "What were you about to say?"

"Well, I was about to say some bad words, but my conscience told me not to."

He's getting the idea.

Even so, I fully expect him to start calling his friends "stupid-head" while shooting them with disintegration blasts from his laser gun, and we'll deal with it as it comes. But his conscience better kick in before he tells some guy at a grocery store that The Mommy thinks he has a nice ... destiny.

January 7, 2003

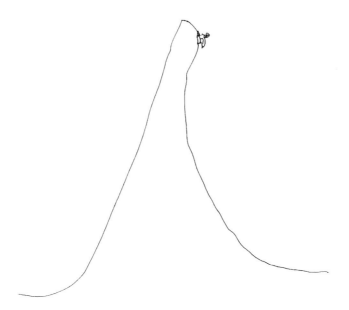

Real Men Proven on Sledding Hill

On the first day of Clarksville's Great Blizzard of 2003, The Boy and I trudged out through the 4.2 inches of snow, bundled up like Russian hunters, carrying a pair of split-open cardboard boxes. We were extreme sledders, looking for some choice slope.

At the top of the hill in our back yard, I decided I'd better take a trip down alone, just to show The Boy it was safe. I jumped head-first onto the cardboard box, knocking the wind out of myself, and skidded to the bottom, collecting a face full of snow all the way down. I stood up, looking like a skinny snowman, and wheezed unconvincingly, "C'mon Boy! It's fun!"

"Daddy, I think we should probably go drink some hot cocoa."

I hauled my cardboard back up the hill and talked The Boy into riding down with me. This he would do, so I sat him on my lap, and with a kick of my foot we were off. The second ride was much better: Instead of The Daddy being encrusted with snow, The Boy was. I brushed him off and told him he did great.

"Yeah, but I think we should go drink some hot cocoa now."

The next day we set out again, this time borrowing our neighbor Dr. Frank's Flexible Flyer sled. I tried it first, just to make sure we wouldn't end up in the Cumberland River. You'd be amazed how well an actual sled compares to a cardboard box. The Boy saw me get to the bottom fairly clean and full of breath, so he agreed to go along on the next trip.

"You should go by yourself," I said. "It's fun."

"But we should both go, then we can both have fun!" he said, proving The Mommy right that I shouldn't look forward to the day he'd listen to reason (it works both ways).

I agreed, but then I did a mean daddy thing. I set him up on the sled, and, rather than climbing on behind, I "accidentally" gave him a push. He did great halfway down, then realized I wasn't there, turned to look and rolled sideways into the snow. I knew what was coming if I didn't act quick, so I ran down the hill, shouting, "Wow! I wish Mommy had seen that!" and "You were so brave!"

"Yeah, I sure was brave," he said, starting to believe it himself.

We climbed back up the hill.

"Daddy, I was actually kinda scared."

"That's OK," I said, suddenly channeling Andy Griffith (pre-Matlock). "Being brave is being scared to do something, but doing it anyway."

"I guess I was brave."

"Yep. Wanna do it again?"

"Yeah, but this time don't forget to get on behind me."

We did. And a couple of times he went down on his own, when Daddy "forgot" to climb on.

I guess some kids come into the world acting brave and some need a push down the slope. Either way, I'm not worried: He climbed back up the hill every time.

January 21, 2003

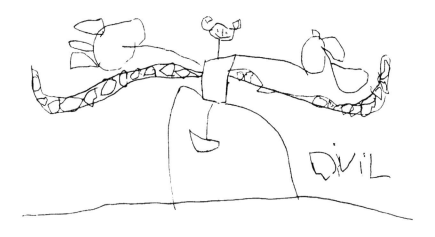

Devil Chases after Daddy's Perfect Day

I straightened my tie and sang a Lou Reed tune as I walked upstairs to wake The Boy.

"Oh, it's such a perfect day; / I'm glad I spent it with you. ..."

It was a perfect day. My usual Sunday routine is to slam my fist on the snooze bar several times, then fly around the house like a maniac so I can be late for church. But this morning, The Mommy and I woke early and refreshed, and lilted from room to room getting ready, relaxing in all the extra time we had before we had to leave.

"Oh, such a perfect day. / You just keep me hanging on ..."

Normally my singing is enough to wake the dead, but apparently not The Boy, who was splayed out like a collapsed skeleton.

After a good jostling, The Boy sat up, rubbing his eyes.

"Here, put this on."

"I don't want to wear this," he muttered, then started crying. So much for the perfect day.

He was still crying when we got downstairs and The Mommy

asked, "Uh, who picked that outfit?"

"Daddy," The Boy blubbered.

"Let's go find something that matches," she said.

"They were on the same hanger!" I protested, shouting between barks from The Dog, who needed to go out. So I took The Dog outside, where she ran loose and peed on her leash.

When I got back to the kitchen after an angry 10 minutes of leash-washing, The Mommy reminded me we hadn't moved her car from behind the house since the day it snowed. I gave up on breakfast and went back outside.

Just as I feared, it had gotten way too cold: The car's battery was dead. I dropped my head to the steering wheel. No church service was worth this; we should give up and get back in our pajamas. Then I remembered something my mom used to say on hectic Sunday mornings, something handed down from a long line of good Methodist women: "It's The Devil trying to keep you out of church, and you can't let The Devil win." I'm Episcopal now, so I'm not supposed to put as much truck in The Devil, but something about that old Methodist admonition stirred me up. I lifted my head off the steering wheel and hoofed up the driveway, started my car and drove it down to the garage. I hooked up the jumper cables, started The Mommy's car, slammed all the doors and pulled to the front of the house.

The battery had set us back another 10 minutes, but with luck we'd still catch the sermon - after we got the kids settled in children's church and the nursery. The Mommy began explaining to the nursery folks that The Baby was ready to fall asleep and ...

"We forgot the bottle," she said.

Driving to the house for the bottle gave me a chance to scream real loud and say words daddies shouldn't say in church clothes. Driving back to the church gave me a chance to think: There's no such thing as a perfect day, at least not when you have kids. Best you can hope for is not to get spit up on, and I'm ahead of The Devil on that score, at least.

January 28, 2003

The Daht Bounces for Pthbbt 'Nah'

The Baby has said her first word. Well, kinda.
It's more like she's come up with her own language, which is actually more impressive.

The first word of this language is "Nah-nah-nah-nah ..." We're not sure how many "nahs" are in there, because it seems to vary by how soon we bring her the "nah," which is babyspeak for "banana," or any other food she happens to want at the moment. And that's usually banana.

Of course, a language consisting entirely of one-word-that-usually-means-banana isn't much of a language (unless you're Anna Nicole Smith), but there's more to it than that. If the "nah" doesn't come soon enough, apparently the speaker is supposed to say "nah" progressively louder until all you can make out is a high-pitched scream that can be stopped only by shoving mushed-up banana in her mouth.

There appear to be two more words in this language, but their usage and meaning are under debate (mainly because The Mommy won't listen to reason). These words are "daht" and "da."

"Daht," pronounced "daht, daht, daht ..." refers to The Dog, the primary source of interest in The Baby's life right now. Why? Well, in addition to being about her size but covered in fur, The Daht often jumps up and licks The Baby's toes while she's in her high chair. This is a signal for The Baby to drop mushy Cheerios, graham crackers or even "nah" down for The Daht to eat off the floor.

"Da" of course means "my beloved father." I know this because when I come home and swing The Boy over my head The Baby shouts "Da, da, da!" until it's her turn to be swung around, which makes her smile and giggle. Now, certain mommies will insist that The Baby says "da" all the time, including when she has a dirty diaper. But this just shows how much she misses her father in the course of the day.

Like most baby languages, this one is also physical. Just like "nah" means "Feed me now," there's a sign for "That's enough, thank you. I'm stuffed and simply couldn't eat another bite." That translates in baby to waving-your-arms-madly-and-smacking-the-squash-filled-spoon-with-your-hands-while-saying-"pthbbt!"

The other physical part of this baby language most of us will recognize: the bounce. For example, when meeting The Daht or Da, or when presented with "nah," The Baby will often "bounce," bending and unbending her spine in a manner not unlike Garth from "Wayne's World." This can be mistaken for actual dancing if she's standing up and leaning on the coffee table, but it is in fact a bounce, and it translates roughly to, "Party time! Excellent!"

With such a clear language already in the works, I don't see any reason to stifle The Baby by making her learn English. Heck, if she's gotten this far by with some repeated syllables and thrown food, she may end up with her own TV show. It can be all about feeding "nah" to The Daht. And that's still more literate than "The Anna Nicole Show."

February 4, 2003

Melodrama Not Enough to Win Parole

My job is to write and edit. The Mommy's job is to raise our family. The Boy's job is to explore how far he can travel down the road to perdition without getting punished. (I've heard they do this when they're 14, too.) Lately he walks right on the edge, for example jumping on the furniture in slow motion or splashing bath water at his sister without actually getting her face wet.

But last week, he not only walked the line, he crossed it, ran another two miles, ate lunch then came back and stomped on it a few times.

The Mommy was sitting on the floor and The Boy was on the couch behind her. They were bantering about something silly, then he flat out smacked her on the back of the head.

Now, there's a couple of ways to deal with this. One is to scream,

"We don't hit!" and slap the kid as hard as you can across his backside. (Don't laugh, I've actually seen someone do that.) Another is to ask the child why he did it and spend a half-hour sharing our feelings, during which time the child just might up and smack you again.

Like most parents we fall somewhere in between.

The Mommy laid out The Boy's full name, followed by the dreaded: "Go-to-your-room-do-not-come-down-do-not-ask-for-a-story-put-on-your-pajamas-and-go-to-bed-good-night."

A 5-year-old can move pretty fast trying to get out of earshot before a mommy comes to the end of a command like that one. He knows it's only going to get worse if he can still hear her when she stops for air.

Once he was gone The Mommy and I did a postmortem — what was up with that? Were we ignoring him? Was it just a playful tap? Nope. He wanted to see what would happen if he whacked The Mommy. Well, we can do that.

Mr. Melodrama cried and cried. He threw in some yells loud enough for us to hear. After awhile The Mommy went upstairs to brush his teeth. When they were done, The Boy said, "Mommy I'm really really sorry I hit you. Can I come downstairs now?"

"Thank you for apologizing, but you have to face the consequences of your actions. You can't come downstairs."

This was his cue for more crying. "Mommy, if you don't let me come downstairs I'm going to cry all night long."

"You can cry as much as you want to," she said, trying to keep a straight face. "But you're not coming downstairs."

"But Mommy," he said, pretending to gag and choke, "I'm choking to death. You're the only one (gag, gag) who can (gag) save me."

"Goodnight Boy," The Mommy said, and almost fell down the stairs laughing.

The Mommy says we may lose our Attachment Parenting license over this, but The Boy got the point. The next day over breakfast, he mentioned how we'd had a bad night.

"I hope you guys don't send me to my room like that again," he said.

"Then I guess you better not hit The Mommy again," I said.

"OK, I'll never do it again."

And if anybody believes that one, we may save a lot of cash on acting lessons.

February 18, 2003

Flying Kissinger Foiled Again

We try to teach The Boy the important things in life: Good manners, the alphabet, how to use the VCR. I often wonder, though, if we're doing this right.

The Mommy and I were talking about a newspaper article on Americans making fun of France, and The Boy piped in that The Mommy taught him to speak French.

"Bonjoo misoo," he said.

Then he switched to what he calls Spanish: "Schmokah da Fayah Dohg." (Translation: Smokey the Fire Dog, which is the only thing he can say in "Spanish.") He's much better, though with Star Wars languages.

"Do you know Jawa?" I asked.

"Ooo chee-gee!"

"What about Tuskan Raider?"

"Haurgh! Haur-haurgh!"

Yep, we've got a multilingual kid.

These are just a few of the things we probably should not have taught him. There are plenty more. After he overheard a report on NPR that Henry Kissinger was going to lead the investigation into 9/11, The Boy asked, "Who's Harry Kissinger?"

"Henry," I said. "He's a super bad guy."

"Can he fly?" The Boy asked.

"Yep," I said. "And he shoots laser beams from his eyes."

"Wow. Harry Kissinger's sure a powerful bad guy," The Boy observed, and for the next week or so he shared this news about Kissinger with everyone he met.

Apparently New York City got wind of this, and Kissinger has returned to his bad-guy secret hideout, laser beams and all.

Some things we've taught The Boy, such as being polite, have a way of backfiring.

We broke him of interrupting us with, "Excuse me? Excuse me? Excuse me? Excuse me?" Instead, he puts his hand on my arm or leg until I reach a stopping point in my conversation and ask what he needs.

This works great. Except when he walks up to other adults and puts his hand on their arm, leg, hip or belly and stands there staring until they ask what the heck he's doing.

And it worries me when he does this because I'm never sure what he's going to say. We'd taken The Dog in for a set of shots, and the vet asked The Boy if he had any questions. The vet and I expected something like, "Why can't I feed her green beans?" But The Mommy apparently has been teaching The Boy more than we thought.

"When will you do the operation where you take out her uterus so she won't have puppies?"

Maybe we should take the hint and stop trying to teach him things like manners, biology and French. But I suppose even if it all goes wrong — even if he grows up thinking Henry Kissinger and Oliver North are conspiring with The Joker and Lex Luthor to take over the world — at least no one will know what he's talking about because he'll still be speaking Jawa.

February 25, 2003

Family Planning Requires a Plan

Remember how last week in this space I made fun of new dads? "Sucker," I think was the word I used.

Yeah, that was pretty funny.

Here's something else that's funny. A joke for you: What do you call people who practice natural family planning but never get around to putting their plan into practice?

Pregnant.

(That flashing neon sign over my head with an arrow pointing down says "Sucker.")

But wait, an astute reader might say, didn't you guys just have a baby?

Yeah, that's pretty much what we were thinking when we saw the purple line on the pregnancy test thingy. And yeah, The Baby will be 18 months old for the birth of The Surprise.

THIS WASN'T PART OF THE PLAN!!!

We want a third child, sure, but we also want to retire to a quiet place on the Gulf and complain about Medicare cuts over a game of Uno — that doesn't mean we want to do it NOW.

Apparently, God wasn't clear on our plan and instead sent us the rush delivery.

So, what does this mean?

This means The Mommy has to unpack the maternity clothes she put away last week.

This means we'll have two kids in diapers at the same time for, oh, about a year.

This means that come October, we'll have running around this house two adults, three children, a cat and a dog. That's a 57 percent spike in our household population in just two years. And the demographics are against the grown-ups.

This means The Dog isn't the only one getting fixed this year.

But some good stuff will come of this.

This means we're forced to buy a minivan. I'd promised The Mommy we'd get one before we had our third child — there's just no way you can fit two adults, three kids, suitcases, toys and baby gear in our car. (Come to think of it, The Mommy was talking an awful lot about minivans last month. You don't think ...? Nah.)

This means, as a friend pointed out in church the other day, I have a designated driver for next nine months. Heck, if we get that minivan she can take us all barhopping.

This means we'll be taking that vacation to Disney World in the spring rather than summer. We promised The Boy we'd go this year, and I don't see The Mommy, at seven months pregnant, waddling through a long line to ride "It's a Small World After All."

This means I get a major new income tax deduction two years straight.

But what this really means is we get to bring a new life into the world. A little sister who might grow up to giggle over boys with The Baby or a little brother to romp in the woods with The Boy. Knowing our kids, The Surprise will have to romp in the woods either way.

It's not the way we planned it, but life is full of big surprises. And in about eight months, The Mommy will be too.

March 11, 2003

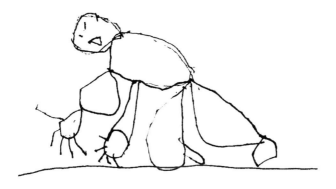

Danger Girl Puts Parents to Shame

Usually when The Mommy calls me at work it's to ask me to buy something horribly embarrassing on my way home. I'd give examples, but let's not compound the problem.

Last week, though, she left one of those messages on my voice mail that begins: "Let me tell you what Your Daughter has done."

It seems The Mommy was in the kitchen trying to re-create some semblance of order in her life when The Boy shouted: "Mommy come quick! The Baby's on top of something she could fall down from and hit her head!"

When The Boy was a toddler, he was Little Mr. Cautious. He would no sooner try to climb down a staircase than try to change his own diaper. Instead he'd stand at the top of the stairs and holler until someone came to haul him down. So he gets kinda panicky about his little sister's stunts. He freaks out when she gets within five feet of the computer ("She's about to electrifry herself!") or has drool hanging from her mouth ("She spit up all over the place!")

But this stunt The Mommy hadn't heard of before. She looked in the den to find The Baby had crawled up a footstool and onto the coffetable — a good two feet off the ground — and was headed for the edge. The Mommy ran in and grabbed her before she took a nosedive to the carpet.

I felt a little relieved to hear The Mommy tell me this, and that she'd let her guard down with our little Danger Girl, so I told her about a minor incident last week.

"Remember when The Baby disappeared and I found her in the kitchen?"

"Yeah," she said, tentatively.

"Well, when I said, 'She's in here,' what I should have said was, 'She's in here banging around on the oven door, which I left open after we finished cooking dinner.'"

There was a pause.

"But she didn't burn herself." There was another pause, and I thought, "I really should not have told her that."

But it turns out The Mommy had an even better one.

"Now you have to promise not to tell anyone this, OK?"

"Sure."

"Last week I had her in the playroom — nice and safe. I had to go let the dog out, so I pulled the baby gate shut before I went out. After about a minute I came back in and could not find The Baby. The gate however, which she has apparently learned how to open, was ajar, and I heard some little noises upstairs. She had climbed the stairs and was crawling around in the bathroom."

I gave her a pause. " ... OK, that's nowhere near as bad as what I did."

"Oh, thanks."

We decided have a little daredevil on our hands. We're going to have to babyproof this house like it's Rikers Island and keep a double watch on our top inmate. If that doesn't work, I guess I can pick up something horribly embarrassing on the way home from work, like maybe a leash just the right size for Danger Girl.

March 18, 2003

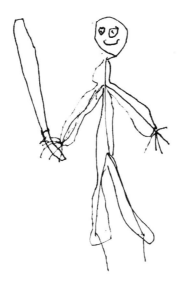

Snips, Snails, plus a Pinch of Jedi Knight

"Daddy, guess what."

"What?"

"Did you know that spiders have eighty fifteen thousand eyes?"

"No! Wow."

"And — you will not believe this down to your toes — flies spit on their food and make it all mushy before they eat it."

At that, The Mommy got up from the dinner table. "I'm done."

Yep. Snips and snails and puppy dog tails. I never bought into all that — that boys are born boys and girls are all sugar and spice. But I have to say, either we're inadvertently raising our son to be a stereotypical boy or they mostly come out this way.

The first signs of this were with his toys. He was naturally drawn to cars and trucks, then seemed hell-bent on smashing them up. We made sure most of his toys early on weren't gender-specific. But he ignored any baby-like or female toys (including girl action figures) and mostly used his stuffed animals as sidekick heroes or sword-wielding bad guys.

When he watches "Star Wars: Episode II, Attack of the Clones," he asks me to fast-forward through the love scenes, which he calls as "the boring parts." He doesn't know yet the term "chick flick," but I think he gets the concept.

He's also learned how to burp on command.

And now we have the ick factor. Most of it comes from watching the Animal Planet channel once a week at Nana and Grandaddy's. Sometimes it gets too much even for me, particularly when the conversation veers to creeping things that creep on the earth.

"Daddy, did you know snakes can swallow ..."

"I don't want to hear about snakes," I said.

"But this one snake can ..."

"I don't like snakes," I said. "I don't want to hear about it."

"But just ..."

"BOY, IF YOU MENTION SNAKES ONE MORE TIME YOU'RE GOING TO YOUR ROOM."

The Boy pondered this for a moment. "Daddy, did you know a tapeworm ..."

"Let's watch Star Wars."

The Baby, on the other hand, is more sugary spicy — showing an interest in girl things.

First of all, she has this thing about shoes. I'm convinced her first actual word (after "I adore my brilliant father") was "shoes." She says it mostly walking around, waving a shoe in one hand, nodding her head, repeating "shoos, shoos, shoos." I think Imelda Marcos spent most of her weekends doing this same thing.

The Baby likes to chew on her shoes as well, not unlike The Dog.

She's shown early signs she's into the homemaker role. She got her hands on a paper towel last week and proceeded to wander all over the kitchen, stopping every few steps to wipe up the floor.

Actually, The Dog does that too, only not with a paper towel.

Now that I think about it, The Baby's more like The Dog than she is like a lady. They both whine when they're done sleeping, they both go crazy when I walk in the door and neither of them are potty trained.

The Boy may be made of snips and snails, but I'm thinking The Baby's got dibs on puppy dog's tail.

April 8, 2003

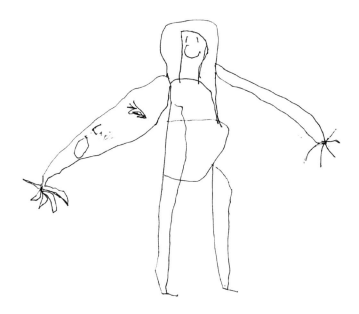

Disney Fun in the Ears of the Beholder

Hey Daddy! You just found out your wife's pregnant and your dog scored an 87 on its obedience school final! What are you going to do now?

I'm going to Disney World!

And I did, actually.

It had to be done. The Boy's 5, and with two little siblings coming up fast behind him, this would be his last shot at Disney for a while. I wanted him to see Disney the way I did when I was a kid.

All the way there I daydreamed about the rides. I couldn't wait to see The Boy's face at the bottom of Splash Mountain.

Then there's The Haunted Mansion. As I recall, I was first dragged into that one by my big sister, who loves to be scared, but only if someone else (i.e., me) is along to hear her scream. The Boy would love it.

And 20,000 Leagues Under the Sea. ... I've always wanted to go on that ride (my big sister must have thought it was dumb or something).

From the opening gates, The Boy was thrilled. Until we got to Splash Mountain. He heard the screams from about a half-mile off, and once he connected those screams to the line we were headed toward, he backed up like a turkey from a chopping block. He did NOT want to fall down the mountain and he did NOT want to get wet.

OK, no Splash Mountain.

Next on my to-do list was 20,000 Leagues, which was right down the path and ... closed. Not just for the day. Not just for the season. It's gone. In fact, it closed about nine years ago, and I never got to ride it. These are the things therapy is made to heal.

OK, no 20,000 Leagues.

"Boy, are you ready to go in the spooky Haunted Mansion?"

"... Is it scary?"

OK, no Haunted Mansion.

So what would we do? Well, the trip was for The Boy, so we let him decide.

Top on his list was meeting the characters. But he wasn't interested so much in posing for a photo and getting an autograph as he was in making conversation. He riddled Pooh with a series of questions, such as "Do you get sick from eating all that honey?" "Is it hard to be a Pooh?" We ended up with pictures of the back of The Boy's head as he interrogated Mickey Mouse and the baboon from "Lion King."

Next on The Boy's agenda was a ride I'd never seen: Buzz Lightyear's Space Ranger Spin. You travel in a three-man space pod through an arcade of targets, using laser cannons to rack up points. We went through twice, and would have kept getting back in line if The Boy had had his way.

It wasn't the Disney I remembered, but then it wasn't supposed to be. It's his childhood, not mine, and that's something I have to remind myself of entirely too often.

Hey Daddy! You just spent 10 hours walking around Disney World eating junk food, studying a map and trying to give your 5-year-old a vacation he'll never forget! What are you going to do now?

Me? I'm going to bed. (Wake me up in five years for a trip to Epcot.)

May 20, 2003

About The Author

Christopher Smith is the 35-year-old married dad of a 6-year-old boy, a 2-year-old girl and a 1-year-old girl. He's the news editor at *The Leaf-Chronicle*, in Clarksville, Tenn. He previously worked as a copy editor at *The Tallahassee* (Fla.) *Democrat* and at the *Daily Home* in Talladega, Ala. Christopher received a master's degree in English from Auburn University in 1996, and went to high school in Haddon Township, N.J. He was born in Athens, Ala. *Daddy on Board* has run weekly in *The Leaf-Chronicle* since May 2001.

Acknowledgements

This book, my column, my life, would not be possible without Kate — my wife and my editor. It's not easy to take someone's work and pick it apart, telling the writer to do more and try harder. But Kate accepted the role eagerly, and has handled it with skill, patience, good humor and compassion. *Daddy on Board* owes a great deal to her insistence on a consistent voice, her high standards for writing and her loving encouragement of the author. I never set out to marry an excellent journalist who could help shape my writing, but it sure turned out that way.

Timothy Smith, illustrator, is an aspiring robotics engineer who volunteered many busy afternoons to help bring this book to life. He specializes in pencil illustrations, occassionally accented with crayon, on a white paper medium. Most of his works are in the genre of space aliens, monsters, robots and Egyptian gods.

Shayne Bowman not only designed this book, he pushed me to publish it. He was also a prime mover in establishing the Web site, www.daddyonboard.com, and in generally encouraging this old college bud to chuck the second-guessing and go for it. Shayne is the co-author of *Designing Web Sites That Sell*, a book on e-commerce web design; *We Media*, a report about participatory journalism; and the whitepaper *Amazoning The News*.

Colophon

This book was designed by Shayne Bowman on a Macintosh using Adobe's Creative Suite software: InDesign, Acrobat and Photoshop. The body text font is Hoefler Text, designed by Jonathan Hoefler. Headline and accent text is Interstate, designed by Tobias Frere-Jones. For more on these fonts, see: www.typography.com.